MW00961678

Follow Your Dog

Follow Your Dog

A Story of Love and Trust

Ann Chiappetta

Cover photo and photo of Bailey with a big stick
©2017 by Pat Weber

Photo of Verona in the snow
©2016 by Cheryll Romanek

Photo of Ann and Bailey on Graduation Day
courtesy of Guiding Eyes for the Blind

DLD Books
www.dldbooks.com
Editing and Self-Publishing Services

Copyright 2017 by Ann Chiappetta
All rights reserved.

ISBN: 1978341679
ISBN13: 978-1978341678

Table of Contents

Acknowledgements

This book wouldn't have been written without the trustworthiness and intelligence of my first guide dog, Verona; her successor, Bailey; and all the dogs I've known and loved who came before them.

I am most grateful for this life, for being fortunate enough to be able to appreciate and benefit from the mutual bond with dogs throughout my life up to this point. I also want to acknowledge the people who know the value of the human–dog partnership. Thanks to my birth family for being there when I began losing my vision, and to my husband, Jerry, who stuck it out with me; to my kids: I am proud of them because both have grown into compassionate and caring adults who understand abilities beyond disability. Thanks to Charlie Brown, the affable and clownish Airedale, who looked into my eyes and allowed me to see a beautiful canine soul, and to all the dogs who enriched my life by trusting and befriending me since I connected with Charlie Brown as a child.

Thanks to all my writing friends and editors. Your support and feedback are more valuable than gold.

Thanks to Leonore and David Dvorkin, my editors and publishing experts, who helped me with kind and skilled guidance.

Most important, thanks to Guiding Eyes for the Blind for so much, most of which is written on these pages and the remainder of which is stashed in my heart.

To my sister and photographer, Cheryll, and her eye and instinct for knowing just what I am imagining and making it happen.

Special thanks to the folks who have helped me in all aspects of my personal, professional, and writing endeavors. You all know who you are; I hope you won't mind my skipping out on a very long and protracted thank–you list.

Introduction

And so, on to the introduction to this book. The idea for it began after I started a blog and wrote about working and living with a guide dog. At the time, around 2010, I wasn't even trying to write a book. It just happened. Blog posts morphed into essays, then into a few chapters, and so on.

I was writing other prose. Many shorter essays and poems were published, too. Yet I felt it wasn't time for a biography or memoir; both my parents were still alive, and I struggled with how to approach them once the words were written, the content of which might cause them emotional pain. Our family was torn apart by divorce and other things. I wasn't sure either of them was ready to be examined by others in, of all things, a book. I worked on a fictional account of growing up, then tried a first-person version of it, and finally gave up. Who was I kidding? I wasn't going to get it published. I was afraid of how my words would affect my family and friends. How did memoirists do it? I was at a loss and put the manuscripts away, moving on to other things.

I concentrated on short works, wrote for a few online magazines, completed non-fiction and poetry for a few years, posting a few short stories and more than a few poems on my blog, www.thought-wheel.com, which got very little feedback.

During this time of what I call writing but not getting anywhere, we said goodbye to our dad, then my mother-in-law, and a few years after that, our mom.

We were in Mom's apartment, getting it ready to be cleaned out, and I was listening to my sister–in–law read some of Mom's journal. I was struck by how well Mom wrote, the beauty of her prose. At that moment, I promised myself that I would honor her memory and get published.

The journey was not overly long, but frustrating. The technicalities of desktop publishing were significant barriers; people I contacted to find out if anyone could help me with the formatting and uploading, etc., were dead ends, and I was about to give up. Then it came to me to read other guide dog partnership stories and find out who their publishers were and follow the route leading to those prospects. I found the email address for Leonore and David Dvorkin, and the rest, as they say, is history.

In closing, I hope you enjoy and are impacted by this book. I hope you learn something about how something beautiful can grow from the soil of loss and suffering. I hope that even if you are not a dog–centric person or animal lover, you will find this book compelling and entertaining. There is not just a spiritual but also a practical merit to the human–canine bond. It has had over 70,000 years to develop and is quite unique. It's not akin to any other relationship, even though it has benefits similar to any other valued animal–person interaction. It is more than just anthropomorphizing your animal to where you believe that your dog will learn how to read someday or that dressing Fifi up in puppy fashion products makes her oh so cute and happy.

The best I can do without drawing from the book's message and spoiling the story is to say that the person and guide dog are interdependent, and the bond of mutual trust is what makes the partnership successful and fulfilling for both. Ask yourself how many people you would trust with your life, and after answering, ask yourself if you would trust an animal with your life.

Unless you are bonded to and live with a working dog, you might hesitate in answering the second part of the question. Let me say here that although I use the phrase "working dog," the words don't explain what a "working dog" really is, contextually speaking. What I mean is a dog that accompanies a person while working or going about activities of daily living. It could be a hunting dog, a show dog, a dog used to mitigate a disability, a therapy dog, or, in fact, any dog that keeps company in a significant way during day–to–day business. It is this unique and powerful partnership that I hope to explain so that the reader can understand and appreciate it.

Thanks for reading.
Annie C.

Part One

Man's Best Friend

George Graham Vest, 1869. Closing argument of Old Drum.

Gentlemen of the jury: The best friend a man has in this world may turn against him and become his enemy. His son or daughter that he has reared with loving care may prove ungrateful. Those who are nearest and dearest to us, those whom we trust with our happiness and our good name, may become traitors to their faith. The money that a man has, he may lose. It flies away from him, perhaps when he needs it the most. A man's reputation may be sacrificed in a moment of ill-considered action. The people who are prone to fall on their knees to do us honor when success is with us may be the first to throw the stone of malice when failure settles its cloud upon our heads. The one absolutely unselfish friend that a man can have in this selfish world, the one that never deserts him and the one that never proves ungrateful or treacherous, is his dog.

Gentlemen of the jury: A man's dog stands by him in prosperity and in poverty, in health and in sickness. He will sleep on the cold ground, where the wintry winds blow and the snow drives fiercely, if only he may be near his master's side. He will kiss the hand that has no food to offer, he will lick the wounds and sores that come in encounters with the roughness of the world. He guards the sleep of his pauper master as if he were a prince. When all other friends desert, he remains. When riches take wings and reputation falls to pieces, he is as constant in his love as the sun in its journey through the heavens.

If fortune drives the master forth an outcast in the world, friendless and homeless, the faithful dog asks no higher privilege than that of accompanying him to guard against danger, to fight against his enemies, and when the last scene of all comes, and death takes the master in its embrace and his body is laid away in the cold ground, no matter if all other friends pursue their way, there by his graveside will the noble dog be found, his head between his paws, his eyes sad but open in alert watchfulness, faithful and true even to death.

Past, Present, and Future

January 2009

It was the second week of class and the coldest night of training. While we were getting into the van to drive here, Jamie, one of our class instructors, told us it was 16 degrees with a wind chill of −5. The night walk was the challenge this time, and it wasn't the first one of the day, either. Our class had already put in a full day of routes; the bitterly cold winds, ice, and snow flurries had been plaguing us for days, and now we were expected to brave it once more, and I wanted nothing to do with it. I just wanted to go back into the dorm and crawl into bed with my hot water bottle. I was mentally and physically wrung out. Part of me just wanted to stay in the van and not face my fear and the horrible weather. I sat in the training van with my thoughts, waiting for my turn. I hated walking at night. I felt dizzy, often stumbled, and had no sense of direction. I wasn't convinced a guide dog could ameliorate the vertigo or the panic whenever I stepped out into the darkness.

I sat in the heated van with a few other students and waited. The students who didn't have any light perception wouldn't be worrying about anything other than how cold it was tonight. The others, like me, who did depend on the light to feel safer, were as edgy as I was, and we talked quietly, trying to help one another through the anxiety.

It was week two, and I was just beginning to feel like I could be a guide dog user. Prior to that, though, week one had its ups and downs. The night walk was supposed to build our confidence when partials like me were expected to depend on our dogs even more.

I was managing to keep the panic at bay, but just barely; I was using breathing techniques to ease the fear, but the butterflies were still there, and I sent up a silent prayer asking for help. I recall thinking, Ann, you are a therapist; you experienced and survived the birth of two children; use your coping tools. It took the edge off a bit. Then it was my turn.

I told Jamie how nervous I was, how dizzy I often felt at night, and she assured me I would be safe and that Verona would keep me straight, even if it felt strange.

"Remember, Verona knows what to do. Just follow your dog. I'll be right behind you."

Earlier, our class supervisor, Dell, had made an announcement at dinner, letting us know that even though it was cold, as long as our walk was under 20 minutes, students and dogs would not be at risk from the brittle, freezing weather. He said that each dog should be wearing boots to protect it from the ice and salt. He also spoke to each of us about bringing gloves, hats, and scarves, and said that those of us with breathing problems should bring our inhalers.

I wasn't even thinking about that, I was so anxious about whether or not I'd trip and fall or worse. I remembered to put my inhaler into a pocket before I left.

The first block was the hardest. I felt like I was in the old *Batman* TV show, walking on a slanted street. Jamie assured me I was walking straight and encouraged me to keep good posture, and it would get better as we went.

We avoided a patch of ice, then stepped off the first curb. I needed my inhaler; the cold made my lungs seize a little, even with a scarf and collar covering my mouth and nose. After putting the inhaler away, I gave the forward command, and we started across the street and found the opposite curb. I was instructed to go left.

The first week of class, I needed extra time to adopt a modified left turn because I was overcompensating and stepping on Verona's back foot. Thanks to practicing left turns, I didn't step on Verona anymore.

I realized we were in town, walking past store fronts. Jamie was describing the stores, the people, and how cold they all looked. I felt the frigid crunch of ice and salt underfoot, the soft clopping of Verona's booties, and the darkness surrounding me. I realized that it wasn't as scary as it once was, and I allowed myself to relax. I listened, opened my senses to the pace of my dog and to the reassuring, sturdy harness handle, and kept walking. I had relaxed, letting my dog stretch her legs a bit and finding a rhythm.

We were going past the ice cream shop, and I was wondering who would be crazy enough to eat ice cream on a night like this, when I heard someone calling to me. "Hey, young lady, want to buy an ice cream?"

My face must have shown my confusion, even if it was hidden underneath a scarf and hat. The voice sounded just like Dell's. I knew he was a jokester, and I decided to take a chance and call him out.

"Dell, is that you?" I called back, but he didn't reply.

Verona took me around a few snow–covered benches and tree boxes and stopped at the intersection. We were halfway through, and I was feeling less anxious.

Jamie caught up with us and we stood for a moment.

"Was that Dell at the ice cream shop?" I asked her.

"I don't know. I was talking to Carrie."

Carrie had come to join us. She was an instructor's assistant and would one day become an instructor, like an apprentice. She was assigned to help the instructors during our class routes and helped like a gal Friday. Carrie routinely helped by taking pictures, making lists, running errands, and so many other things it made my head spin.

I let it go, even though my bullshit meter was going off. I had to let it go, right? I was blind and couldn't prove it really was Dell, which was annoying. We made another left turn and finished the route. I'd forgotten about the ice cream man by then.

We stood at the van. I was cold but so happy. I'd done it; Verona had done it. I had faced my biggest fear, walking at night, feeling the vertigo and the retinal star bursts floating across my eyes, hoping it would go away, and then feeling it lessen as we walked. The harness handle and Verona's guidance had kept me from panicking. Her steady pace and gentle pull had kept me grounded.

I wanted to kneel down on the ground and kiss Verona, tell her thank you for helping me face my fear of night blindness. I didn't, though. I would save my true and tearful gratitude for later, in the privacy of my room. I did this every night before turning in—petting her and talking to her, saying so many things, mostly through tears of relief, joy, and even grief. Verona was helping me process the complicated emotions of leaving behind not just the anxiety of being unable to see and rely upon my vision, but also finally putting my poor view of myself away forever, thanks to her calm and accepting manner and unconditional regard. I was getting back my confidence, and it was more than a little overwhelming.

I realized Jamie was talking to me, and I returned my attention to what she was saying.

"You did great," said Jamie. "Not one wobble," she added. "Are you still nervous about walking at night?"

I thought about it, petting Verona's head. "Not as bad as with a cane, that's for sure. It's still scary, but at least now I feel less dizzy. Holding onto the harness and feeling the dog helps keep me from feeling like I'm falling."

She asked if my breathing was okay, and I said yes. It was the first time I had resorted to my inhaler, but it was only 16 degrees out, after all.

"I want you to check in with the nurse first thing tomorrow. I want her to make sure you're okay to go out on route tomorrow morning."

"Okay, but why? I feel fine."

"Just a precaution, that's all," she said.

I nodded, got into the van, and was very happy to feel the warmth of the heater as I peeled off the scarf and took off my hat. Verona curled up beside me, her head on my foot. I remember thinking how nervous I was only 30 minutes before, and how good it felt to not feel it anymore. If I couldn't see at night, so be it. I now had a way to stay safe when I did need to go out in the dark, and it felt reassuring. I still wasn't keen on doing it arbitrarily, though, and I knew I would have to keep working on the anxiety and vertigo each time I did decide to take on the night.

I spent the remaining time in the training van listening to music and talking quietly with the other students. I knew Verona and I were shaping up to be a great team, and I may have been smiling in the dark warmth of the van until we started up and drove back to the dorm.

Coke Bottle Bottoms and Solitude

What was life like before getting my guide dog? Maybe the correct question should be, what was life like?

It was a mixture of frustration, fear, and isolation, tempered with a fierce desire to be as independent as possible. Since the age of five, I had struggled with progressive vision loss from a degenerative retinal eye disease called retinitis pigmentosa. The fluctuation of what I could see on one day and not the next was the most debilitating. I did what I could on my own and asked for help only in an emergency. I spent a lot of time alone, and some of it was lonely.

There were things I didn't see accurately, and it often left me feeling unsettled and somehow responsible. There were also times when I missed something completely due to being visually impaired, and after I was told or found out that this had happened, I was often devastated, embarrassed, and sometimes physically sickened by it.

There were times, over the years, that I hated being asked if I needed help, times I pretended I could see better, times when I turned the hate inward. It took a very long time to stop this, and one of the only times I felt whole was with my dogs.

But let me tell a bit more about where I grew up and how being a kid with poor eyesight groomed me to become a better person.

I was born in 1964. Living in a quiet harbor town in a solid middle–class neighborhood kept me safe from most of the harsher social situations. I remember the river down the street from our house. It became the first place where I sought solitude in my surroundings.

I sneaked down to the river one sultry afternoon in midsummer, knowing that if caught leaving the backyard, I'd be in trouble. I was forbidden to go alone, but my mother and sisters weren't around, so I took it upon myself to walk down the street and find out why the other kids got in trouble for going there.

I crossed the street and walked over the bridge. I turned right at the end of the rusted iron rail and stopped at the top of the path leading down the embankment. To my five-year-old eyes, the way down looked very steep, but I was determined to get to the bottom. I planted my sneakers and rode them down on the loose dirt and gravel, pinwheeling my arms until I stopped. I coughed, spitting the grit from my nose and mouth. I remember looking up through the dirt cloud hanging in the humid air and wondering if I'd make it back up. The path to the street looked awfully steep. But I was in a different world, now, far below the hot sun and the people-hungry flies and yellow jackets.

I found a large, flat rock and sat, smelling the dankness and listening to the burbling water sounds. It was busy, yet lacking the anxiety of home, which was rife with adult emotion. My young mind recognized the value of this place, and at once I knew it would soon become my refuge of choice. Climbing back up the embankment meant going back to the house and its problems. From that point forward, the rock by the river was the place to escape.

I found a baby snapping turtle at the river, taking it home and keeping it as a pet until it climbed out of the tank and died in one of my sneakers. I hunted salamanders, marveling at the vivid orange stripes contrasting with the black body and the creamy belly before letting them go squiggling from my hand, back under a rock or rotting log. I poked centipedes, mindful of the pincers and how quickly they could crawl. I caught crayfish and watched the local trout but couldn't ever do more than pet them. Part of me didn't want to ever catch them. I didn't even trouble with frogs or toads; they were boring.

The river symbolized a safe, quiet sanctuary, far removed from the scary challenges of what was happening inside and around our house. Once my parents revealed they were divorcing, my ability to trust people evaporated. Nature and the river restored some of the continuity I'd lost. The flow and cycle of the seasons were more acceptable in my confused mind. It was easier to coax a squirrel to eat from my hand than to ask my parents to play a game or help me with my homework.

After graduating from grammar school and moving on to middle school, I returned to the rock near the river often, sitting on it and losing myself in the world below the street in the old neighborhood. Back then, there was a family of beavers trying to dam the river, and a giant snapping turtle, and crayfish you could snatch up in the eddies lining the bank. Nature didn't care if I wore Coke bottle–bottom glasses. In fact, I could lose myself in it, and that was the best thing about nature—you didn't have to do anything except enjoy it. I was part of it, not being singled out for being different.

When I was 10, my father showed me how to fish, and I would take my pole and tackle box and walk down to the estuary lining the harbor and cast for hours. I caught and released small fish. I absorbed myself with reading about animals: how they lived, how they died, and most important, how they behaved.

I was different. I observed people and kids, often declining to engage because I didn't want to disappoint them when I missed a ball, couldn't see in the dark when playing tag, or cause my team to lose because of something having to do with my poor vision. Worst of all was if I knew someone else was uncomfortable around me because I couldn't see. I watched, listened, held back.

It wasn't that I didn't try. The anxiety of not being able to see like everyone else was always there, just under the surface of my thoughts. If I lost or broke my glasses, my panic was intense. If someone asked why my glasses were so thick, I'd blush and get embarrassed and tongue-tied.

When I broke or scratched them, I was berated for it, my father gritting his teeth, telling me I was thoughtless and irresponsible. How did I expect him to pay for new glasses that cost three weeks' salary? How did I think it felt to ask for a loan to pay for them? I'd better be more careful and not ever let it happen again, he would say. After this barrage, I would cry and often go months without my glasses being repaired, getting by with tape and bent frames. This taught me to view my vision loss as a weakness, a bad and shameful thing.

After a few years of being berated for the rough treatment of my glasses, I began to hide how bad my eyesight was and avoided visits to the eye doctor, insisting I was "the same." I learned to downplay how poorly I could see, not wanting to be a burden to my parents.

I was very insecure about my vision loss for other reasons, too—being teased at school, having to choose not to participate in sports because my glasses would fly off and break. Or, if I did take them off, I was useless because the world was too blurry and it made me dizzy. The worst was to finally get up the courage to play and fail because I couldn't see; this feeling has stayed with me, and even now it is difficult to overcome.

I proceeded through these formative years perceiving myself as broken, less than. This is not to say it wasn't worthwhile. I had to constantly challenge this perception of myself and my abilities, recalling, often much later, that overcoming the poor image of myself was part of personal growth.

I learned about self-preservation, pride, humility, humiliation, and not giving up or giving in to despair, although I came close to the last of these many times. Sometimes it was due to my disability, and sometimes it was just being a young person trying to navigate the social intricacies of life.

I recall, while growing up, there was one other visually impaired girl who lived across the street from us. She, too, kept to herself, read books a lot, and was shy. I used to see her sitting on the porch, a book inches from her face, just like me. My father would push the book away from my face and say, "Don't hold the book so close. You will ruin your eyes."

I would sigh and hold it farther away and wait until he left the room, then put it back where the words weren't blurry. I often wondered if the other girl's father did that to her, or if they allowed her to hold the book as close as she needed to.

Even though I wasn't very friendly with this girl, it made me feel a little better knowing that I wasn't the only kid with vision problems.

My family would try to get me to look up when I was walking, or stop squinting when reading, sewing, or reading the newspaper. I looked down all the time. It was the only way I could see with some measure of acuity.

We were all ignorant. It wasn't until I was handed a white cane at age 28 and instructed to lift my head and square my shoulders that I finally won back some of my confidence. I spent most of my life up until then looking down at the ground because I could only see out of a small portion of my constricting visual field.

The times when I didn't feel insecure came when I was with nature, like at the river, or with animals. I read as much as I could about them. Audubon and other encyclopedias were my favorites. I tried sounding out the Latin names, loved listening to bird songs, and watched all the shows on television.

I found acceptance and peace in other creatures, and I

especially loved my family's cats and dogs. I wanted to learn how to train animals, found ways to go horseback riding, and read about how the military trained dogs. Every time I went to a circus, my thoughts focused on how the trainers made the animals perform. I wanted to be one of them, to learn to communicate with them. I thought that communicating with an animal was easier than with a person. I also felt that trusting a dog was more reliable than trusting some of the people in my family at the time.

My family was experiencing divorce during these formative years, and for me and my sisters, it meant that we just couldn't rely on our parents being honest or rely on the things we used to for stability.

I escaped into books.

One thing that helped me persevere was a book given to me by my uncle Harry. It was called *A Girl and Five Brave Horses*, by Sonora Webster Carver. It's a biography of the daredevil horseback divers who performed a show on Atlantic City's Steel Pier in the 1900s.

The author was blinded when she and her horse, Red Lips, slipped on the diving platform and hit the water badly, injuring both of them. Sonora suffered detached retinas, resulting in eventual blindness. Undaunted, she kept diving. I read that book a hundred times over, wishing I could get to do something that exciting, pairing up with a brave horse, careless of the consequences. By this time, my self-esteem wasn't being fostered, and I ended up turning away from taking chances because I believed I would never be good enough.

I was broken, a four-eyed fat girl who couldn't see.

Unconditional Regard with Four Paws

When we adopted a dog, I began to understand more of why I loved animals and how they helped me gain back my self-regard. My love blossomed when we adopted Charlie Brown, a one-year-old, undocked male Airedale. He was gentle, loyal, and smart. It was CB who stimulated my wanting to understand animals. He gazed directly into my soul with almond-shaped eyes I thought more human than canine. I felt a thrill at that moment, as if he and I shared something special. He expressed more in that first, unwavering inspection than I'd ever been able to bear from a person, and although it was strange, it was also thrilling to me.

From that first time our eyes met, he protected me, made me laugh, and never judged me, even though I made mistakes.

One year after we got him, I asked for a stuffed, life-sized Lassie dog for Christmas, having seen one in the FAO Schwartz toy catalog. I watched the TV show *Lassie* and wrote Santa that I would like one. Christmas morning, I saw it, a life-sized Collie plush toy, under the tree in a down position. It had a red patent vinyl collar and gold chain leash with a red patent handle and brush to match. I was thrilled. I took it everywhere and groomed its lush, faux fur coat, wondering at how calming it felt, almost as good as petting a real dog, like CB.

One warm spring day, I finished brushing Lassie and left her on the picnic bench, called away by something else. When I returned, the Collie had been ripped apart, and CB was sitting there, his mouth covered in stuffing and fake Collie hair. I cried out and shooed him away, grabbed the ruined toy, and ran into the shop. My grandfather was in there, and I ran to him.

"Look what CB did to Lassie!"

"We told you not to bring it outside," he chided.

"It was CB, not me. CB was bad."

He looked really mad, and I felt confused because I took very good care of my toys. Just this once, something bad had happened, and I didn't think it was my fault that CB tore up Lassie.

"Do you want to punish him?" Pop asked, the mad look gone, another look replacing it.

This confused me even more. I looked over at what remained of Lassie and made up my mind. "Yes," I said, thinking he would tie him up or not give him dinner.

Instead, Pop grabbed a hatchet and called the dog, who came over, wagging and looking at us expectantly. Pop took him by the tail and positioned it on the chopping block used to cull chicken heads.

"Tell me how much," he said, raising the hatchet.

Stunned, I watched him raise the sharp blade, unable to move, trying to comprehend what he was going to do. As he raised the hatchet, I found my voice. "No! CB didn't mean it!" I cried out, pulling CB's tail out from under his hand.

I stood in front of the dog. "It isn't his fault," I said.

He lowered the axe. "You will take better care of your toys?" he asked, lowering the hatchet.

I hugged CB and nodded my head.

My grandfather walked back into the shop.

I learned then to be responsible, not to take out my anger and disappointment upon others, and to be accountable for my mistakes.

This is just one life lesson I was able to grasp, prompted by an interaction with a dog. CB didn't hold a grudge, get mad, or stop being my friend. He did seem a little ashamed about tearing up Lassie, though.

In his book *Marley & Me*, John Grogan writes about the ultimate dog, the one no other dog can measure up to, no matter what. CB was my perfect dog. And I miss him terribly. I can remember his dark, soulful, almond–shaped eyes, how his wiry eyebrows expressively moved up and down, how his soft muzzle tickled my hand and face, his doggie smell, and most of all, his carefree and happy nature.

Our family had a lot of animals over the years, but I still compare all our other dogs to CB. It's probably because CB was a good dog, and a good dog, in a natural and free sense, is a gift to have in one's life. In the following pages there will, of course, be other beloved dogs with whom I've shared life and adventure and who have taken up space in my heart. Each has shown me how to continue keeping my heart open even after saying goodbye. These dogs all contributed to developing both appreciation of and passion for the canine and human bond. It is to the love of these dogs who have gone before that I dedicate the next few stories.

Earning and Learning Doggie Style

When I first met my husband, he owned a female Pit Bull named Blackie. She was a challenge, and I continued my personal journey of love and acceptance with her. She was 55 pounds of jaw and muscle, jet black accented by white-tipped tail and feet. A white star finished her elegant markings.

Jerry, my husband, found her abandoned, starved, and beaten along a road with another pup while he was stationed down South during his enlistment in the Navy. The first pup died a few days later. Blackie survived, but she was horribly traumatized and never successfully made it to being a trustworthy dog with anyone but our family. She went after other dogs, nipped a few friends and family members, and only respected those who didn't back down or who were "okay" and approved by either Jerry or me as part of the pack.

Our bonding was odd, to me, and a bit funny. To this day, I still laugh over it.

I was walking down the hall of Jerry's family apartment, and out came Blackie, growling. I stood my ground, grabbed the broom, which was only an arm's length away, and promptly bopped her on the butt with it.

She stopped. Her expression was a mixture of shock and shame.

"Don't ever do that again, you hear?" I said, looking at her.

She turned her gaze away and slinked to me, her tail wagging apologetically.

After that day, she came to me happily, began obeying my commands, and sometimes ran to me and ignored Jerry.

We eventually moved into our own apartment, and thus began our true bonding time. I fed, walked, and brushed her, and took her to the vet for vaccinations. Jerry and I ran her in a field in back of our building, and she loved it. She was fast, and I wondered if she wasn't just a little bit of Greyhound, too. She was so happy when she ran free; her eyes shone, and she smiled, appearing relaxed, which she did not often show, being a very reserved dog.

She was a scrapper, though, and we never took her among other dogs, having had encounters that ended up with biting and fighting. We purchased a spiked collar for her as a precaution. It warned other dog owners to steer clear and would protect her neck if she did get in a dog fight.

Despite her dog aggression, Blackie was a good judge of character. She turned away a man at one of our parties, backing him into our bathroom, her teeth bared, hackles up. We asked him to leave and afterward found out she had caught him trying to steal wallets from our guests, rifling through the pile of coats and purses in our bedroom. Another time, she nipped a friend's husband and eyed him the whole time he was in our house. He was later convicted of molesting children. She felt protective of another adult friend, and every time he came over, Blackie would curl up under his chair. We learned that if Blackie liked someone, the person could be trusted, but if she showed her disfavor, we also kept a watchful eye.

The tender part of Blackie shone when our children were born. She slept under their crib, lay next to me as I nursed or fed them, and never hurt either of them. She let them take kibble from her bowl and feed her by hand, too. Her lips would graze the chubby little hand, and the giggling resulting from the touch of her whiskers was the sweetest sound.

Blackie was also my first animal to euthanize. Jerry wanted nothing to do with being there, his tough guy exterior disappearing when he knew it was time for her to go. So I carried her in, already knowing she was in distress. Earlier in the year, she had begun showing signs of kidney disease. We did what we could, but it wasn't enough. The only thing that kept us from feeling truly horrible was her age. She was 14 and in pain, and we believed that her quality of life would have left her in an undignified state.

On that day, we knew this would be her last visit. The vet assistant scooped her up, and I followed him into the exam room. After a thorough exam, the vet put a hand on my shoulder, confirming what I already knew.

"We could give her some fluids, but due to her age and condition, you wouldn't have much more time with her. She's in advanced kidney failure and in pain. It would be best to let her go."

I stood next to her, seeing how tired she was. Her eyes seemed to say she was ready. She couldn't stand up on her own and had lost control of her bladder. I wanted her to live but knew I needed to give her a dignified passage even more than my selfish need to keep her going. If I had known then how much harder it would progressively become to say goodbye like this, I would still have done it. But each time wrenches a place in my heart that no words can express.

I nodded and stayed with her while they sedated her. Once her eyes closed, I stroked her sleek head and graying muzzle, fondled those little tipped ears, and whispered that she was loved and that we would miss her so much. After her last breath, I unbuckled her collar, walked out of the exam room, signed the cremation agreement at the desk, and left.

She could have died in that box on the side of the road, but she lived and lived well. With her quirks and broken but sweet and protective personality, Blackie taught me to accept the limitations of others. She helped prepare me for what was to come.

Blackie

Two for One

We waited until my kids were a little older before adopting another dog. Maybe we waited a little too long, though, because we ended up with two.

It began with a Polaroid snapshot. We were ready to take on another canine companion and family pet, and I asked Jerry to spread the word at work to see if anyone else knew about puppies. It was springtime, the best time for puppy finding. One night he came home and handed me a Polaroid. Back then, I could still see close up, and I held the photo to my nose. I was struck by the one brown and white pup who was looking up at the camera, his eyes bluish green and glowing from the flash. I thought of CB and smiled.

I gave the photo back and said, "I want the one that's looking at the camera." I went back to stirring the dinner pot.

Jerry put the Polaroid back into his work shirt, then said, "I'll see if they can bring them down over the weekend." He added, "Let's meet them all before you pick one."

I didn't challenge him, but my gut told me that the pup with the flashing eyes and the tawny brown and white markings was the one. I couldn't wait to find out for sure.

That Saturday afternoon, Bill and Sue showed up, set up an octagonal baby gate, and deposited six eight–week–old puppies.

Jerry and I watched them. Then I asked if I could step in with them. Sue nodded. As soon as I was among them, the pup who was looking up in the photo trotted over and began sniffing my foot. I made a kissing noise, and he looked up at me, his little head tilting as if to say, "What's that?"

I gently lifted him into my arms, and he began kissing me, grunting. He settled down soon afterward, and my heart tripped a little bit. I wanted this puppy.

I looked at Jerry. "This is the one I want."

Jerry made a face, then pointed to the largest pup. "What about that big white one?" he asked Sue.

She shrugged, picked it up, and put it in Jerry's arms. It grunted and didn't seem very happy about being held.

"Can we handle two?" I asked him.

He thought about it. "I can if you can," he said, that familiar and defiant twinkle in his eye.

I refused to give up my puppy, and he was not giving up his, either.

He turned to Sue and said, "We'll take both,"

After months of house training, crate training, and leash training, Rocky and Gunny became part of our family.

There were moments when Jerry and I would look at each other and say, "This is nuts. What were we thinking?" This was almost always after mopping and cleaning up after them or after feeling frustrated with Gunny, the larger one, when he chewed up another doll, toy, or stuffed animal.

Luckily, the kids were still young, so we made a room for the puppies in our dining room, and this made it much easier to housebreak and crate train them both. We named the room the puppy room because we blocked it off with baby gates and it was large enough to give them play space and keep them from getting into trouble.

Gunny did have a penchant for chewing the walls, eating an entire hole in one of them. He also chewed the handles off a cabinet, ate through our metal cable TV splitter, and would eat anything on the ground outside.

Rocky, thankfully, happily saw the sense in chewing his

bones and stopped chewing on Jerry's leather boat shoes.

He did, however, have trouble controlling his bladder and often peed in excitement on Jerry's work boots when he came home at night. I thought it was funny, but after Jerry got mad and made Rocky even more likely to pee, we devised a plan after calling our vet for help. Thanks to Dr. Winokur, Jerry would come home, ignore Rocky, go straight into our bedroom, and close the door to undress. When he emerged and sat down, he would call the dogs over and only then say hello. It worked. After a few months of this, Rocky's excited leaking stopped.

Fully grown, Gunny was 90 pounds, tall, shaggy, and white, with odd black splotches which reminded me of an Appaloosa quarter horse I once rode. When he walked, his tipped ears bounced, and it made him look very goofy. He resembled a Collie.

Rocky was a rich, tawny brown with white markings. A white diamond marked the back of his neck, above the collar, and his toes and tail had white tips. He had the slope of a Shepherd, and his tail crooked at the end. His best feature was the black mask around his eyes, the reason we named him Rocky, like a raccoon.

Early on, we had trouble with Gunny. He was nervous, often hiding, and would growl when bothered. His lip would curl when he was meeting strangers or strange dogs, too. He had bad knees and would yelp whenever he ran or played with other dogs, often limping. We didn't have the money for surgery, so we got him on joint supplements and pain relievers when he would reinjure himself. I began obedience training with Gunny, and after months of frustration, found some success with a prong collar and a head collar. He was not a trainable dog for an amateur like me, though, and while I did manage to instill some discipline, he didn't advance like Rocky. It was a constant source of concern for us, as he weighed in at 90 pounds and stood 26 inches at the shoulder.

Rocky, however, didn't seem to suffer from poor joint health and was a great family dog. He began guiding me even before I could put a name to what he was doing. He took the lead and kept me on the sidewalks, stopped at curbs, and found dropped items for me. He was obedient and sensitive, and he loved all of us very much. He even liked cats. Gunny just wanted to chase them.

I knew Rocky was special when we took him camping near a lake in Delaware. We had a friend keep Gunny because he was just too anxious to be trusted in an outdoor environment. We also didn't want him to injure his weak knees. Rocky made us proud. He river–walked with us off–leash, bounding ahead, checking on the kids, and making sure we were all together. He stood sentry in our tent, emitting a low growl if the critters came too close. He didn't bark, and when a fierce storm blew in, complete with lightning that hit a tree nearby, he never flinched. There is a photo of my daughter and Rocky standing in our campsite. She said she remembers that trip as one of her favorites because we had Rocky with us.

A few years after the boys turned five, I noticed Gunny was scratching at his ears. Soon after a vet visit, a series of illnesses began to appear: first ear infections, then occasional intestinal issues, then skin issues, and finally he became lethargic and gained 15 pounds in a few months. The vet tested him for thyroid problems after he collapsed during a routine walk. He was diagnosed as hypothyroid and was prescribed a dose of Synthroid. He improved within months, his coat and hot spots healing, his ear infections no longer an issue, and his digestive problems lessening.

It was then I noticed his irritability. When I directed him to get off the bed or couch, he would grumble. Then the grumbling began to sound more like a growl. Then, one night, I walked past the bed where he lay and put my hand out to stroke his head as I passed, and he snapped at me. I reprimanded him with a word, and he growled at me. I thought about making him get off the bed but didn't want him to be even more aroused, so I let him be until it was time to go out. I was shocked. He actually went to bite me—this gentle giant whose mouth was so soft, he couldn't even play tug without losing.

While his physical symptoms improved, his mental state was decompensating. Over the next few months, he bit and menaced my son and menaced Rocky, who had no clue what to do and ran behind me for help a number of times.

After weeks of this behavior—growling at us, snapping at me, and once menacing a neighbor who had known him since puppyhood—I said I couldn't keep him unless there was a way to keep everyone safe. When I asked our neighbor to recall how he approached her and menaced her, she said he was asking to be petted. Then he looked up at her. His eyes dilated, and he lifted his lip and began growling. She slowly removed her hand and looked away, telling him to lie down. This was troubling, as she was his walker, too, and had known him since he and Rocky were pups.

I took him to the vet, who agreed to evaluate him.

Meanwhile, I searched journals, coming across a study on behavior problems in dogs who were prescribed Synthroid. Also during this time, our new vet asked a behavioral specialist to evaluate Gunny for adoption. The person who evaluated him said he could not be adopted due to his unpredictable nature— that he would spend his life in a crate most of the time, and that there was little hope. The vet and I read the article I found stating that 10% of dogs prescribed Synthroid for hypothyroidism became mentally unstable and had to be destroyed because of aggressive behavior. We even considered Prozac, but even this medication couldn't be guaranteed to curb the aggression and fear biting.

Jerry and I were beside ourselves with frustration, and we were losing hope that Gunny would be able to continue living with us. He was a large dog, and this was the deal breaker. We had young children and had already been through the limitations brought upon us by Blackie and her quirks. The difference was, though, that Blackie never menaced our family. If we couldn't find a new home for Gunny, we did not want to think about the other decision.

Then the decision was made for us. The worst possible thing happened. He bit my seven-year-old daughter. He chased her down, and as she tried to escape him, he bit her in the back. I wrenched him off. He tried to go after me, but I got a dining room chair, backed him up into the bathroom, and slammed the door.

I ran to my daughter and pulled off her shirt. Thankfully, although he had grazed her skin, his teeth had only punctured her sweatshirt. I hugged her, and we both cried. When I opened the door to the bathroom, he came out, docile and friendly. I kept him separated in his crate until the next day. That night, he growled and snapped at Jerry, and it was then that we made the decision to give him up to the vet. We were out of options.

The next day, Gunny was being kenneled with the vet. We were trying to find him a new home but came up short. No one would take a chance on him. The veterinary staff said he was okay when in his crate but they could tell he wasn't "solid."

I went and spent time with him five days a week, walking him to a local park, sitting under the trees, and crying. I knew he couldn't stop taking the medication; without it, he would die a horrible, slow, agonizing death. The other choice was keeping him mildly sedated, in a kennel, and muzzled when out of his kennel. After experiencing his aggression toward all of us, I just couldn't put our family through it.

I knew we had to let him go. A life in a cage was no life. We struggled with the humane decision; we talked it over with our vet; we made another attempt to adopt him out with a single person who had no other pets. After four months, and bringing him home only to see his aggression reappear, we all agreed that euthanizing Gunny was our only choice.

It was Rocky who taught me that the bond between a dog and his person runs deep. It was Gunny who taught me to make the decision to let go with both the heart and with humane sensitivity. He was only six years old.

* * * * *

One day, six months later, I looked over at Rocky, and he looked back at me, and I saw something in his eyes. It was pain, fatigue, or something like pain. I went over to him and petted his head, and he closed his eyes and went back to sleep. I told Jerry that something was wrong with Rocky. Jerry said that we could take him to the vet the following week.

Four days later, he vomited, and a stringy black substance hung from his mouth. I wiped it away and went straight to the vet. After a bariatric test, a mass was detected. My heart sank. I knew it was cancer. The vet said it could be anything, and she wanted to do exploratory surgery to make sure it wasn't a blockage or foreign object. We consented and Rocky went under the knife.

"Honey, it's cancer," Jerry said.

I froze, unable to move. I had called him between graduate classes to find out Rocky's prognosis.

"It's bad, honey. His stomach and colon, big, black strings of it."

I wanted to puke, but took a breath instead. My beautiful, stoic dog, suffering like this for who knew how long, and I only got a clue by seeing the pain in his eyes. Boy, I felt like shit just then.

Rocky came home with a huge incision. The vet couldn't remove any of the tumors, calling them aggressive and knurly. The biopsy identified them as the most aggressive canine sarcoma.

Rocky had only a few months to live.

"Give him whatever he wants; keep him eating until he won't. When he refuses food and water, it's time to bring him in," the vet said, handing us a bag with syringes, liquid prednisone, and pain medication.

When I brought Rocky in to be euthanized, he weighed only 30 pounds. I easily lifted and carried him into the vet's office. Jerry was so upset, he stayed in the car and cried.

Rocky lay on the exam table, looking at me, those almond–shaped, soulful eyes, so much like CB's, telling me it was okay. "I'm ready, let me go, I'm in so much pain." I told him I loved him, that he was the best dog ever. And then he was gone.

I don't know how long I sat there, my head on his chest, crying, but eventually I got up and left, feeling empty and angry. Rocky was seven years old.

Looking back, I now understand why I experienced these losses. Losing my dogs prepared me for the Phoenix, my baptism by fire. I was going to lose my sight and then risk my heart again by applying for a guide dog.

Gunny and Rocky as puppies

Part Two

Living the Blind Life

When we first adopted Rocky and Gunny, my vision was in a stable place. However, after Gunny was euthanized, my vision took another plunge, and I lost more of my visual field. It was 2006. I no longer read large print, and I had bouts of color blindness, as well as ocular migraines that often left me exhausted and sick.

I was working on a master's degree in family therapy and felt unsafe when walking the college campus at night. One night, I had made it down the long curve of steps that led to the street, had crossed the street to another parking lot, and was trying to find the door to the building. It was late and windy, with a coating of rain on the ground. The reflections made by the wet ground were disorienting. I was walking carefully across the lot when my cane fell into a drain and got stuck in the grate. I stumbled and went down on a knee, my bookbag landing in a puddle.

I managed to unstick the cane tip and get inside. My pants leg was ripped, and my hands were scraped and bleeding. I wanted to cry. I was just so angry and upset. I didn't want to struggle like this anymore.

I ended up being 20 minutes late for class and almost didn't go because I didn't want anyone to see me so out of sorts and feel sorry for me. But I sucked it up and made it to class anyway.

Not one person asked me about the rip or the wet bookbag—which was a good thing, because I think I would have cried if asked.

A few months later, just before I graduated, in May 2007, I was walking down the street to class. My cane did not detect a construction barrier across the sidewalk, and as I stepped into the barrier, I almost flipped over it. I rebounded and ended up on my butt, winded, my ribs bruised and my face flaming in embarrassment. I wanted to sink into the cracks of the pavement, and I hoped no one had noticed what had happened. I ended up backtracking and crossing the street to the other side, where it was clear.

As I tapped along, I thought, If I had a guide dog, that wouldn't have happened.

A few friends in the local blindness group I joined had dogs, and I asked them about how the dogs helped them. One person recalled how her dogs, over the years, had kept her from falling in holes, had helped her cross busy streets safely, and had helped with other tasks that I thought were impressive. Even so, I thought that I still wasn't blind enough, and soon the idea that I could get a dog was buried while life and family kept me occupied.

Finally, in late 2007, a few months after I graduated, upon the urging of my therapist, Bill, I contacted a local guide dog school and applied for a guide dog.

The field instructor came to my home and interviewed me. She also videotaped my cane skills. Then she blindfolded me and asked me to walk the route again. I panicked, felt dizzy, and ended up stumbling into some bushes. I was humiliated and felt like the worst blind person ever to walk the earth. All of my skills meant nothing with the blindfold.

What the instructor and I both failed to note was that I was experiencing a side effect of retinal degeneration. I still have this symptom. It's commonly called vertigo. Night blindness is the cause, which results in disorientation and dizziness when the retinas spasm with the lack of light and send back the wrong message through the optic nerve to the brain. The misfiring of information causes pain, dizziness, and disorientation.

By the time she had me following her on the Juno walk—holding onto the harness handle and coaching me as she pretended to be the dog—I felt better. I closed my eyes willingly and let her take me back along the route. I remember saying to her that that was the first time since losing my sight that I felt free.

When she informed me, at my door, that I wasn't ready for a guide dog, I burst into tears, saying, "How can you do this? You show me what it feels like to finally walk again in a way I haven't in years, and now you tell me no?" I ran inside, crying.

Unfortunately, even after I asked for a review of my Juno walk, the admissions committee also said no, that I needed to wait until my vision got worse.

The rejection left me feeling depressed, grief–stricken, and unable to look forward to ever finding a way to regain my independence. I kept thinking, How much worse does my sight need to get? How much better of a blind person do I need to be to get a guide dog? I had already spent two years learning cane skills, going to college to earn a master's degree, learning how to use a computer with speech, so many things, and now I was being told I wasn't blind enough? I kept rehashing all these defeating thoughts over the next few months, feeling more and more that my chances of ever getting a guide dog were slipping away.

Bill, my therapist, would not allow me to give up and helped rally me by urging me to do two things: get a complete retinal exam with a visual field measurement, and apply to other schools, in addition to reapplying to the school that had denied me. He said that the former would give me an official confirmation of what I already knew, that I was indeed blind enough to get a dog, and the latter would help by not letting the opinion of one school or person allow me to lose hope. This advice couldn't have come at a better time.

I had been receiving regular individual therapy sessions to help me cope with my vision loss. When the guide dog school rejection came, I became even more depressed. I was angry and felt unmotivated and isolated. Jerry had gotten a new job as a U.S. Immigration Officer and was away on training, which lasted 16 weeks. This was pre–9/11, and U.S. Immigration was a separate department in the government. Jerry's training included learning Spanish, which was why the training was so long.

I was bringing up my kids alone, depending on my family for help. I didn't want to overuse my in–laws and felt very conflicted and trapped.

We were just coming out of a difficult financial period, too. I barely had enough cash to get the essentials, and I felt responsible for this. If I weren't going blind, I would be working, and we wouldn't be so cash poor. Becoming a guide dog user would give me a safer and better way to travel while looking for a job, among other advantages. But the rejection was devastating, and I just couldn't face reapplying after such a negative experience.

Not only was I struggling with the realization that I wasn't blind enough to get a guide dog and missing Jerry's support and helping out with the kids; I was also struggling with losing more of my declining vision.

Retinitis pigmentosa is a progressive eye disease affecting the retina and the light–sensitive cells lining it. According to the National Eye Institute, RP, as it is commonly called, is a group of rare, genetic disorders that involve a breakdown and loss of cells in the retina, which is the light–sensitive tissue that lines the back of the eye. It is a progressive genetic disease and has no cure. It affects each person differently, so the prognosis is unknown. To make it even more difficult to understand and accept, the particular disorder I was diagnosed with is one of the rarest types, a double recessive gene that can skip generations and be carried until triggered. How or why it is turned on is a mystery. One theory is that I was born with weak retinas, and the RP is the most readily identified symptom.

I would experience a few years of stable vision, then a year of progressive loss. I would get dizzy, see weird star bursts and explosions of light across my eyes, and get migraine headaches. M eyes would ache if I strained them with too much reading and close-up work. I often found it uncomfortable to be outside in the sun in the summer, and the reflection from the snow during the winter was painful. Sudden onset of vertigo and dizziness during extreme light changes, or lack thereof, is also a symptom of RP. I wasn't even aware of this side effect until the guide dog school instructor blindfolded me, resulting in the vertigo and disorientation.

At this point, during the time that Jerry was away, I was going through one of these losses. I couldn't take the kids to the playground without help. I had fallen and tripped over so many things, it seemed that I was sporting bruises or sprains every day. I'd even cracked my nose on the back of a chair, not seeing it when I bent over to pick up a toy. I saw stars, just like in cartoons.

Being able to talk to someone who understood what I was struggling with helped. Bill Dale was the best person to give me back some hope. I worked with Bill for three years, and when we finally decided to end therapy, I entered graduate school and later became a family therapist. My time with Bill was a transformative experience, and I am glad of our time together. He is one of the reasons I decided to become a family therapist. He coached me through a very dark period, and after more time than I'd like to admit of feeling sorry for myself, I built up enough confidence to begin believing I could overcome this thing called blindness.

Also at this time, I found a free course through the Hadley Institute for the Blind about guide dogs and how to prepare to apply for the application process. I took the course and would recommend this to anyone considering a dog.

While I am writing about the Hadley Institute, I want to say that this was another very important piece of my readjustment during the early years of vision loss. I found that I liked distance learning programs and excelled in all of them. In 1998, I received the award for Student of the Year and was invited to the school in Winnetka, Illinois for the ceremony, along with a few other award recipients. I was able to meet my instructors and read aloud a poem. I still keep in touch with one of the moms I met, too.

But let me get back to the guide dog story.

It was 2008, and we were past the money problems. Jerry was now a Customs and Border Protection Officer, and I was also working.

I was 41 and looking forward to using my master's degree as a family therapist, getting back to work, and no longer relying on federal disability benefits. I had been a Social Security Disability recipient since 1993, when I was declared legally blind. While it was a much-needed source of income for me, I also felt like I was on the dole, akin to being on public assistance. Much of this kind of thinking came from my parents and the social stigma of being helped by government funds, but it was also the final plunge into accepting that I was "disabled" and needed the government to supplement my income because I couldn't support myself. The day I called the SSI office and informed the caseworker that I was gainfully employed and no longer required SSD, he congratulated me and welcomed me back into the world of the working class.

* * * * *

I was over losing Rocky and Gunny, and a new dog was in our lives, a Beagle mix named Nikka.

I wanted to think that all these animal experiences were preparing me for the ultimate bond, but still, I could not quite believe that. At some level, the little girl with the insecurities of vision loss doubted I would ever work with a guide dog. I still believed that I wasn't worthy enough, trustworthy enough— and, worst yet, blind enough.

Rehabilitation

I was declared legally blind in 1993, just after the birth of my first child. I lost my job, and worse, much of my confidence.

I began the long and painstaking process of learning how to live as a blind person. I returned to school, practiced my cane skills, and challenged my skills by traveling as much as possible. I learned how to use a personal computer with text-to-speech and magnification technology. It took 10 years, during which my vision declined, leaving me no choice but to adjust as my vision worsened.

By now, I was working with another mobility instructor in Yonkers so I could learn the bus routes and immediate surroundings. I had put the dream of being with a guide dog away, giving in to the attitude that I would never be blind enough or good enough to have one.

Thinking back, being shown how to work with a dog and then having it taken away was one of the things that made me a better guide dog handler once I was given the opportunity to show what I could do. While being rejected like that was horrible at the time, it made me work harder to make sure that the next time I applied, I wasn't going to be turned down.

The orientation and mobility instructor had met me at my home and had met Nikka, the Beagle mix we rescued following Hurricane Katrina. We were testing out a route to the bus terminal when he said, "You have a dog at home."

I nodded, concentrating on keeping my cane lined up with

the outside edge of the sidewalk.

"Have you ever thought about applying for a guide dog?"

I stopped, then recounted being rejected two years before.

I could hear the smile in his voice when he said, "I think you're blind enough, and your travel skills are very good."

I smiled back. "Really? You don't know how good it is to hear someone say that to me," I said, trying to swallow the lump of emotion.

By then, I had all the reports from the retinal specialist stating that I had less than 5% of my visual field and that my vision was 20/650 in the better eye, with only motion and light recognition in the other. I was now in the final stages of retinal atrophy. My eyes were dying, but this meant my chances of being accepted into a guide dog program were better.

What a juxtaposition, I thought—being excited about being blind enough to apply for a guide dog. Most folks would cringe in fear, but I was feeling as if a new door was going to open.

* * * * *

I applied to the first school once again, and another on the West Coast. Both schools responded at once and set up Juno walks again.

It had been a little less than two years since the horrible rejection with the first field instructor. When the new one called me, I told him about it, and he said, "No blindfold for you, then," and the anxiety lifted.

The instructor from the school on the West Coast said the same thing, and both home interviews and practice walks, also known as Juno walks, were great. I held onto the harness handle and once again felt free.

Also, as mentioned earlier, after the rejection by the first guide dog school, we adopted Nikka. Nikka came into our lives six months after we lost Rocky and Gunny. The house was empty of loving, furry faces, and we all needed to heal our broken hearts with a new dog. We had planned to adopt a Greyhound from a rescue facility in northern New York. On a whim, we visited our local animal hospital, the same one that helped us get through our awful experiences with Rocky and Gunny. The animal hospital boarded dogs and cats ready for adoption through a rescue program in our local area called Pet Rescue, www.petrescue.org.

Jerry and I met the first dog, a Newfoundland mix, black and gentle. He had been abused and still required surgery to remove air gun pellets under his skin. We said no to him. The second dog was a large, young Lab mix. She was so excited, she jumped on us and knocked over the visiting room chairs. After understanding she needed a house and yard, we passed her up, too. Jerry and I spoke with the staffer, explaining that we wanted a dog a bit smaller and less energetic. She said she had one more dog we might like.

As soon as we saw her, we were smitten. She was a black and tan Beagle mix, with the Beagle attitude, and submissive to a fault. She weighed about 40 pounds, was a year old, and looked as if she'd recently nursed puppies. In any case, she was good with children, wasn't housebroken, feared loud noises, and was a Hurricane Katrina rescue. She was picked up, found wandering the highway after the storm, and destined for the high kill shelter in Georgia. She saw us, licked my husband, and showed us her belly. We were in love.

I trained Nikka, acclimating her to the suburbs, a crate, and leash commands. She mastered most of them, but never got over fear of loud noises, rain, and storms. She ruined my area carpets, urinating on all of them until I threw them out and crate trained her. Within two weeks, she was fully house trained.

She had PICA, an anxiety condition resulting from being sheltered for so long. She chewed my handmade afghan blanket given to us after Rocky and Gunny died. She chewed through sleeves that were left draped over our chairs or the couch cushions. I went through two fleece blankets and a comforter and threw away so many socks with holes that I lost count. She did not chew any shoes, but she loved getting into garbage and used paper goods. Even now, she will pluck a tissue from the box with her teeth, abscond with it into the back of the dog kennel, and eat it. She ate an entire pizza, jumping up on the dining table and helping herself. Let's just say that at first, Nikka was a very anxious and resourceful little dog.

When I left for the 28-day, on-campus training at guide dog school, she pined for me, and when I heard about how she moped and lay at the front door, I cried. I felt so guilty about leaving her and worried how she would adjust to my new dog.

Before that, though, Nikka healed us all with her funny, affectionate personality. Imagine a black and tan dog with a small head, a funny-shaped body, a front end lower than the back end, large front paws, and smaller back feet. She is definitely a Beagle mix, from her motivation for food to her baying and barking. My favorite part of her face is the two brown accents, what I call her "eye dots," common to the black and tan breeds. They are just the best and give her personality. She has a big personality for a 40-pound dog; she puts her butt in the air and places her head between her front feet and demands to be petted. When she is satisfied with that, she flops over onto her side, bays once or twice, and goes belly up. Very cute.

She did okay on vacation. She swam like an otter and loved to dig holes in the sand, too. As of this writing, Nikka is 13 and is still spry and sassy.

Kibbles and Pouches and Leashes, Oh, My!

It's been over eight years since I packed my biggest suitcase and rode up to Yorktown Heights. It was January and had been cold and snowing since before Thanksgiving. I packed two pairs of boots, an extra winter coat, thermal underwear, and a hot water bottle, among other things. I was nervous. In part, my doubts were based upon the negative experience and rejection when I first applied for a guide dog. Sure, since then the interactions had been much improved, but I just couldn't help thinking that I'd be asked to leave if I screwed up, if I acted in a way that I wasn't supposed to act—a.k.a. not blind enough.

I didn't want to encounter any patronizing attitudes, and yet I would have overlooked that if it meant achieving my goal of coming home with a guide dog.

Looking back on how I felt at that time, I was still developing my coping and sense of self after losing vision. The self-doubt and self-pity were still there, ready to bubble up should I feel like I was being criticized or if I failed at something. I still thought of myself as a bad blind person, as someone who still needed to perfect living the blind lifestyle. Heck, I had been told I wasn't blind enough, and this fear of being sent home without a dog was what kept me up at night.

Yet I packed my suitcase and took the chance that the

potential and drive were there, and as I lifted the overstuffed, giant black monster of a suitcase into my mother–in–law's minivan, I was not taking no for an answer. During the drive, I kept telling myself that I was not going home without a dog, no matter how hard it was going to be. I was not going to ring the bell.

On that brisk and sunny Sunday in January, we arrived at Guiding Eyes for the Blind in Yorktown Heights, New York, 40 minutes from my home in New Rochelle. I was met by the class supervisor, Dell, and taken to my room. Carrie, the IA (instructor's assistant), gave me a quick tour of my room and the inside of the building and said dinner was at 5 p.m. I unpacked, got my computer set up, and was blissfully unaware that my life would not be this quiet again for another month and would never be the same again.

January in New York is usually blustery and cold; just my luck, 2009 was one of the coldest and snow–blasted seasons since Y2K. We often awoke to temperatures below 20, with early snowfall from a few inches to accumulations of a foot or more. One week, we were lucky to have it reach 25 during the day. We were chased home early a few times to beat a fast–moving storm, and the third weekend, we got a Nor'easter that dropped two feet of snow over a four–hour period.

I was chapped in places I didn't think I could get chapped and was wind–burned on my face, lips, and hands. We used hand warmers and drank a lot of hot drinks, and I personally went through one big tube of petroleum moisturizer, two pairs of boots, and three sets of gloves. It's hard to explain to anyone who hasn't trained with a service dog, and more specifically a guide dog, what it's like. I can say it's life changing, life affirming. At various times, I cried, felt exhausted, exhilarated, doubtful, happy, and grateful. Instructors did not patronize, allowed us to make mistakes, and, with non–judgmental ease, corrected our errors. Our instructors supported us, made us work hard to achieve what they knew we could, and helped us through some rough training plateaus. It was, and still is, a highly disciplined and regimented program. The staff knew just how to make it look and feel effortless most of the time, but I can tell you that it was one of the hardest ordeals I've ever undergone and one of the most hard-won of all my achievements.

Here is an example of what we were expected to accomplish on any given day: up before 6 a.m.; take care of ourselves and our dogs; do daily obedience; dress and eat breakfast; then get packed up for the day and pile into the training van and drive to the off-site training lounge in White Plains.

I often called the loading-up into the vans the Keystone Kops scene: controlled chaos. We had to work out who entered first, who wanted which seat, etc. After the first week, it was routine, but at first, it was something to learn how to do and do it well. The vans were the 15-passenger Econolines, with captains' seats and lots of windows.

As Murphy's Law would have it, one dog would not want to get into the van. For our van, this was my dog's (Verona's) sister, a petite yellow Labrador matched with an older woman. Talk about a stubborn dog! When she did get in on her own, we would cheer. Many times, she would be helped in with a scoop of the foot by an instructor. She would step up, then just stand there, and eventually an instructor would gently push her up and forward, making her step all the way up into the van.

Then there was the dog pile. The van floor was cold, so the dogs would shift and move and lie on one another to have as little contact as possible with the floor. This caused some disagreements, but none of it was very much more than doggie grumbling. I think the people got more upset than the dogs. Dogs will be dogs, no matter how well trained they are.

Once we had disembarked into the training lounge, which was in a well-maintained, three-story house in downtown

White Plains, New York, complete with seating for a large class, trainers' offices, and other amenities, the instructors told us the day's training schedule. They changed the walk schedule every day, so sometimes I went first, and other days I went last. We relieved and watered our dogs while we waited for our walk. Two walks were accomplished each day, weather permitting.

Lunch was provided. It was hot and included soup, an entrée, drinks, and dessert. While we ate, we were also able to practice navigating ourselves and our dogs into and out of diner–like booths, something I found very helpful, being someone who likes to go out to eat.

We also practiced other techniques, like learning how to position and slide your dog beneath a chair. This is an essential part of the lifestyle. Learning the technique and then using it in public helps both you and your dog understand just how important it is to apply the responsibility of working a dog, and how good technique goes a long way when interacting in public with your dog. The basic gist is to help your dog stay under a chair while you're sitting at a table. This keeps the dog under control and out of harm's way. I can't tell you how many times Verona or Bailey would be under the table or chair and someone would remark, "Wow, I didn't even know you had a dog down there!" That's the point. A service dog isn't supposed to draw attention at times when you don't wish them to, like when dining out, working at a desk, etc. The waiting room is another place where directing your dog to lie quietly under your chair is a good option.

Guiding Eyes made us practice the steps until our dogs would follow the command, pivot, and step backwards between our knees and slide themselves under the chair.

While much of the training kept us practicing many of the same routes and actions, we all had our challenges. Some of the class members were new and learning it all for the first time. Others were retraining and took much of the training in stride, but the retrains sometimes had to leave old habits behind and learn new techniques and commands. The first–time handlers had to learn to trust and follow the dog, something vastly different than holding onto a person's arm or using a white cane.

Sure, there was also some downtime; we sat in the main room, exchanging jokes, news, and other conversation. It was 2009, the first few years after the introduction of smart phones, and many of us had them— playing games, making short calls to home, and listening to music or audio books.

Then there was Larry. He was a volunteer who made corny jokes and gave out candy bars. He sat with each and every one of us, marveling at our good times and bad times. I will never forget his caring and kindness during one of the most emotional times in my life. He made me feel normal and confident and kept me grounded with his frank and warm personality. When I trained with my second dog, Bailey, I asked about Larry, hoping to see him again. I was given the bad news that he had had to stop volunteering because his wife was not doing well and needed his care. He is one of those folks I will never forget and will always think of, wondering what happened to him, how he's doing, and so on.

After lunch, another training walk, and a quick wrap–up, we piled back into the vans and drove back up to the campus. Once back in our rooms, we had just enough time to unpack, feed our dogs, relieve them, and hup it up to dinner. After dinner, we attended the evening's lecture.

Sometimes we had extra down time, and we watched a movie, learned dog massage, were instructed how to stretch with a yoga instructor, learned how to groom our dogs, and even got a chance to make a pair of earrings with a lady who came in and taught us how to make jewelry. I still have those earrings. They match my eyes, and I named them my Verona earrings.

After that, we gave our dogs another opportunity to relieve, then it was lights out. I usually filled up the tub and soaked the soreness from my leg muscles, filled up the hot water bottle, and hit the sack. I didn't have the chance or the energy to worry about anything else. I think that was a good thing, too.

Getting Acquainted

I opted for a training date in January because I knew Jerry would have help from his mom while I was away. The kids were off until the second week in January, too. This meant it would be easier for all of them until I returned with my new dog. Jerry would appreciate not having to get the kids up for school, make lunches, and find a way to get them after school.

I had also asked for a January training date due to my work schedule. I was only able to take the four weeks required for training during January because there was a natural gap between the winter holidays and the resuming of the last half of the school year. I was a youth program coordinator, and I couldn't go at any other time.

Back in 2009, a new student was required to stay at Guiding Eyes for 26 days. Currently, most training programs for new students vary from the full 26 days to 10 days, depending on the program. As of 2016, the writing of this book, the major guide dog schools all meet the needs of new and returning students with programs that are well-designed and flexible and go from a full 26 days to everything in between, including home training, depending on the school and availability of the instructors. Whether you find yourself wishing to train at home, on campus, or a combination of the two, there are programs for that. Some schools meet the needs of students with additional disabilities, such as being deaf or having orthopedic conditions. If you are reading this and are thinking about applying for a guide dog, my advice is to not rush into a decision, apply to more than one school, and remember that you are the consumer, and your needs may be a good fit for one school and not others. Some other suggestions are to call a school and ask to speak to another graduate. Most schools will refer you to an alumnus who can answer your questions. Also, if possible, visit a school. If a school has open graduations, attend one. If not, ask to get a private tour. Some schools live stream graduations or offer YouTube clips about the school and the training program.

At the end of this book, there is a list of the guide dog programs in the U.S., as well as other links for agencies and groups promoting the guide dog lifestyle. I have included them because I believe in the power of knowledge and networking when we are faced with such an important decision as applying for and working with a guide dog.

Training Hurdles

The third day of training, I stopped at the corner and put down the harness handle.

"What's up?" asked Jamie, my instructor.

I'd been struggling with not stepping on my dog's feet when turning left, and now she was not turning left and was backing up to avoid me. I was frustrated and overwhelmed.

"I can't do this," I cried. "I can't help stepping on her. She's going to hate me."

It was cold, my snot was freezing on my face, my new boots had broken, and my confidence was just as frozen as my body.

Jamie patted my shoulder and gave me a tissue. "You're doing fine. This is just a blip. Tonight we'll work on your turns. You'll see; in a few days, this will be nothing,"

I wanted to believe that. I didn't want this sweet, gentle dog to put up with my clumsy ineptitude. "But what if she won't work with me anymore?"

"That won't happen as long as we make sure it stops," she said. "We'll stick to right turns for today, okay?"

I snuffled and nodded and spent the rest of the route working on other tasks. I couldn't shake off the gloom and doom that I was going to go home without a dog, and worst of all, be responsible for ruining a dog because I was an unworthy idiot.

Verona was unlike any other dog. She even surpassed Rocky and Charlie Brown. Let me tell you all how I met a dog that became my new ultimate dog. Once you've read my poem, you'll understand my fear of failure.

Verona

I wait for the knock
Once it comes my life will change forever

Since I arrived
For two days and nights

For my entire life until now—

I've waited
Unprepared
Searching

I sit on the bed
Wondering how it will feel an hour from now
And go numb with nerves

Questions scroll across the marquee of my mind
What will she be like?
Will she like me, learn to love me?

The hot red letters of doubt scroll past
Can she guide me?
Will I be able to trust her?

Then the knock comes and my heart jumps
"Come in," I say
Hoping I can open my heart with as much ease as the
    door.

I hear her nails click on the floor
I put out a hand, touch her head
She licks me, tail wagging
"Ann, this is Verona," the trainer says

I don't really know what to say or how to feel
But her presence soothes me

"Aren't you a beautiful girl?" I coo as the trainer leaves
We sit on the floor together
The marquee of doubt vanishes
The blocky, red letters fade
Replaced by a message of calm, canine acceptance
Dressed in ebony

She settles her head in my lap
Each stroke of my hand
Strengthens the hope, quiets the fear
The questions dissipate with the knowledge
—Stroke by stroke—
That she is the one who will lead me

January 2009

Verona

Dog Day

Before dog day, there were some preparations we were expected to undergo.

The first day of training was Monday. We were issued new leather leashes, stiff and unused. The leash is what keeps you and your dog connected when the handle isn't in your hand. The leash is what some call a police lead, a long strip of bridle leather fitted with sturdy, stainless fasteners and rings. It was equipped with a large snap hook at one end and a smaller snap hook at the opposite end. A large O ring near the dog's end and a smaller O ring at the handler's end made it convertible from a short leash used for working to a long leash for relieving your dog. The leash is relied upon for many different commands and reinforcements and, yes, corrections.

Early on, when I asked whether or not a correction with the chain collar was mean to the dog, I was asked to put the collar on my wrist, and the instructor gave a quick snap. She said that my corrections should be like that, a quick tap on the shoulder, never meant to hurt or choke the dog. It's a way to remind the dog of what should be done, a "sit" or "down," for instance. It isn't a punitive action, just a reminder to do what is asked at the time. It's important not to slip the collar on upside down, or it will not release quickly and can hurt the dog's neck or choke the dog. When holding the collar, make it look and feel like the number nine. I use this to remember: The nine configuration is fine, and the six configuration sticks.

This explanation demystified so much for me in terms of dog handling. I hoped I would come away knowing not just *how* to do this dog–handling thing, but also the *why*, the reasoning behind it all, and this gave me the boost I needed to pay attention and do my best.

The night before dog day, we were gathered in the lecture hall and told the name and breed of our new dog. When I was given her name, Verona, I didn't know what to say. This is it, I recall thinking, and the delay and the look of surprise caught me some teasing later on.

Wednesday was dog day. We went to breakfast, attended lecture, and practiced obedience with the instructors playing the role of the dogs. They made sure we were holding proper position and that verbalization of the commands was good. We were given an hour of free time.

At lunch, the wait began.

* * * * *

By the time lunch was over and we were all told to wait in our rooms to meet our new dogs, I was unable to sit still. I got coffee, I did some laundry, I made some phone calls, and I checked email.

I spent the entire time waiting for the knock at my door, breaking in the leash while going over the snippets of video of other first–timers meeting their dogs. It just made the waiting even harder.

Magic in Black

The moment Dell brought Verona into my room was unremarkable on the outside. He quietly led her in. We clipped and unclipped our leashes.

"Just get to know one another," he said. "No commands or anything. Keep it low key, okay?"

I nodded, unable to speak. I was feeling the lump of emotion take over.

Tears rolled down my cheeks as Dell left. The emotions roiling inside were difficult to control, though. I tried to watch television while Verona sniffed around, then settled next to me on the floor, her head resting on my thigh. Sitting on the floor with her was more comfortable for her, even though my butt went numb after the first 15 minutes. But I didn't care about it because I wanted to be there for her. I wanted her to know that I was depending on her as much as she was going to depend upon me, and she was probably confused and maybe even a little bit sad. Her world was being shifted again in a very short time. She had made the transition of being brought to the school by her raiser to bonding with her new instructor, and once she was settled with that, she had to make one more transition, to me. That's a lot to put on a dog, and yet ever since the first guide dog was trained in the early 19th century, it has been happening successfully and changing lives for the better.

I made a promise to her that I would do my best if she did her best, and I got a snuffle and a lick to seal the deal.

There were growing pains. For example, when Jolene entered the room, Verona would stand up and try to get to her. Jolene was the instructor who had finished her harness work, and when Verona would try to get her attention, I'd say, "Oh, she's making moo-moo eyes at Jolene again." This would make us all laugh.

Some dogs were just doggone stuck on the trainer who finished them out. Some weren't. Some dogs were aloof for a few days while adjusting to the new handler. Some were bonded well after only one day.

Verona was aloof for almost three days. On the fourth day of training, while we watched television before bedtime, she rolled onto her back and let me rub her belly. That was when I knew, unequivocally, that she had made the transition to me as her handler.

From then on, the trust and bond began to build. She was such a sweet and sensitive dog, and at first I made some mistakes at overcorrecting. Once we worked around it, though, I could just jingle the leash, and she would listen to my verbal commands.

But all this came later. Let me tell you about the first time she turned us away from danger.

OMG!

Our first solo walk was on the second day of training. I recall it clearly.

After half a block, Jamie stopped me, unclipped her training lead, and said, "You're on your own. Finish the route." She stepped back. "If you need anything, raise your hand and stop. We're only a second away," she added, fading into the background.

I didn't have time to panic. It was day two. I knew we had to cross one street, make two left turns, then find the training lounge. How hard could it be? But I wanted to raise my hand right then and there and say, "Are you nuts? I can't do this alone!" Then, thankfully, I remembered that I traveled all over with a white cane, and that made me feel a little better.

I took Verona's handle, looped the leash under my fingers, and gave her the forward command.

Prior to reaching the main intersection, where we would turn left, we stopped at a side street with a down ramp. Verona stopped; I praised her and gave her a treat, then listened to the traffic so I could judge when it was safe to cross. Verona began to sidle left, and at first I corrected her. Then she jerked me out of the ramp and out of harm's way. It took what seemed like forever for my cold, muddled brain to register that she had just kept a car from backing into me. She pulled me to safety, and I almost didn't listen. The car pulled off and I praised her, trying unsuccessfully not to cry as we crossed the street. That day was the day I knew we would be a great team.

I sucked it up and finished the route, screwing up left turns, but finishing the route safely.

By Friday, we were handling the left turns much better. It was after our first solo walk that I broke down on the corner. After that, I met with Jamie every night for the next three days and practiced my footing. Looking back, I wonder what the heck was wrong with me. I don't do that anymore.

The hidden jewel in this story is that Verona, bless her heart, didn't let me down. She adjusted and worked just as hard as I did, and we took on my clumsy turning as a team until we overcame it. That's why she is the best.

Part of the Family

While researching the content of this book, I read other books about the folks who live and work with a guide dog. I was, and continue to be, struck by the passion each author has for his or her dog and by the professional and caring examples of the school or program in which it was trained. The heartfelt gratitude is one feeling I identify with, as well as the feeling of acceptance during training.

What I found was lacking—which was perhaps a bit disturbing to me, being a mental health professional—were reflections regarding how the person's family reacted or responded when the team came home. It's not that there wasn't anything written regarding the topic in training lectures or the other books, but that there wasn't enough—at least, not for me.

At the end of week two, the class was informed that the local students could get visitors on Sunday. We were also told that if we wanted to go off campus, our dogs had to stay behind. The instructors explained that if something happened while the new team was out without the benefit of an instructor, it could be permanently damaging to both the dog and handler. I was fine with having Jerry and the kids come up to meet Verona, and I couldn't wait to call him and let him know.

There was so much buzzing around in my head after I hung up with Jerry. I knew I'd have to put some serious boundaries in place with my kids. My daughter, April, was 10 and testing us. My son, Anthony, was great with animals and would listen to the rules. I was on the fence about Jerry regarding boundaries and listening to the rules, but this visit would help me assert them before going home—an advantage, for sure.

I met them in the lobby and introduced them to the instructors. Then we walked to my room. As we approached, I turned and said, "The instructors don't want the dog to get too excited, so I have her on the tie–down. You can say hello, but no excitement."

This was met by three differing opinions, of course.

Jerry said, "Okay."

Anthony said, "I can do that."

April followed with, "Why do you have to keep her tied up?"

I wasn't going to answer, and we had already walked into the room. As soon as Verona saw them, she got up and began wagging. I heard all three of them start talking at once.

"Oh, my God, Mom, she's so pretty!" And, "Honey, she looks so smart." And, "Mom, can't you let her off the leash, just for a minute?"

I gave in like a cheap pair of shoes, but only for 10 minutes. The kids sat on the floor and soon had Verona belly–up and getting rubs. I took the moment to hug Jerry and cry a little into his shoulder. He asked what was wrong.

"It's just so overwhelming, this whole thing."

"You're not changing your mind, are you?"

I laughed and wiped my tears. "Not for a billion dollars."

I let the kids and Verona have a little bit more than 10 minutes. Then I settled her, and we went to the coffee room down the hall to get drinks and a snack.

The visit was short. When they left, I missed them terribly, but that was tempered by the fact that my family would be coming back for graduation the following week.

Bold and Beautiful, Woof!

The final week of training, Jamie told me I could choose what I wanted to do. She referred to it as freestyle and encouraged me to find routes and locations I wanted to experience, ones that weren't necessarily in the regular program we were following.

I thought about it and made the choice to do a bus route in White Plains and end with some orientation at the White Plains bus terminal. I was working in Yonkers and wanted to be familiar with the bus platform I'd need to transfer to in order to get home, in case I needed an alternate way to travel, instead of using the Paratransit bus. We also worked on safely entering and leaving a revolving door and doing a little more country work, which is walking on a road safely without the benefit of sidewalks.

Verona was a star, and I realized that her memory for retracing routes was top notch. In fact, ever since I first realized she could find her way out of a maze, I relied upon her to perform backtracking many times over the years. For example, she expertly found our car in a parking lot when our group was lost on a confusing college campus, picking the correct red SUV, which was parked next to another red SUV. Many times, she led me back to a seat in an airport, restaurant, or waiting room, which left me humbled and amazed at her ability to make fairly complex decisions for a dog.

The most confidence–building route we undertook during

training was Manhattan. Since there were only nine students in the last week of class, we split up, and half went on the Metro–North train to Grand Central Terminal, to the restaurant, and half rode the vans in and took the train back. I was riding in and walking a route back to the station. Jamie was my individual instructor. Each student had one instructor; the one–to–one ratio is wonderful.

We met the other students and instructors at the restaurant and ate a great meal; then I walked from 91st to 59th Street. It felt like I could see again. We were just part of the pedestrian traffic. Verona was great, and once we entered the subway station, she took it all in stride. When we boarded the Metro–North train, she slid in under the seat and promptly fell asleep.

I rode the train lost in my thoughts, still wrestling with how much my life had changed since dog day. I wondered where this new path would take us, and while thinking all these things, I too fell asleep.

The Finish Line

Friday, we had a relaxing day. We were encouraged to play with our dogs in the indoor area. Verona loved the squeaky toys, galloping in circles. She loved to play fetch, too, and would chase a ball for as long as I would throw it. I found out later that she also loved Frisbees and was a good catch.

After we played, I groomed Verona, then caught up on some laundry and began packing. I'd be going home the next day, after graduation. Jerry and the kids, my sister, and a few colleagues planned to come up for graduation. I asked for a ride home so Jerry and I could get help introducing Verona to Nikka.

Class pictures were taken after lunch, and then our vet visit was scheduled. I found out all about my sweet Black Labrador. I'd also be meeting her puppy–raising family after graduation.

I was a little nervous about it. I knew nothing about them until the day before we were due to meet. I got all verklempt when I thought about the unselfishness of being a raiser and hoped I met their expectations. I knew what it was like to lose a pet to the finality of death, but thought that to voluntarily raise them and then give them back was something I just couldn't understand, even though I was grateful for it.

Earlier, I mentioned feeling very conflicted about leaving our pet dog, Nikka, for the month–long training. It was a constant worry for me, too. My gut told me that our homecoming would not be all roses and champagne. This intuition would turn out to be correct.

One of the points I want to make is how complex the transition from being a cane user to a guide dog handler is—not just for the handler, but also for the family as a whole, both good and not so good.

The acclimation to other pets is probably the most nerve-racking; at least it was for us.

Jolene packed us up and drove us home. That was one of the warmer days; I think it reached 35 that day. The 40-minute ride was uneventful, and Verona snoozed in the back, behind my seat.

Before departing from Yorktown Heights, Jolene showed me how to work Verona into and out of the back seat, as if it were a taxi or car service. As I opened my legs to let Verona get into position between them and sit, I thought, So long to my pencil skirts.

Jerry and the kids, along with Nikka, were waiting for us outside when we arrived. Verona led me to them, and she and Nikka got acquainted. Then we all went back into the apartment. I took off Verona's harness and leash, and the moment both dogs were free, Nikka began barking and trying to nip Verona's back legs. It wasn't aggressive; it was as if she was trying to chase Verona out of what Nikka considered "her" home. I could only imagine what she was thinking: First Mom goes away, and just when I was happy to see her, she has another dog with her. How dare she betray me!

Jolene watched the interaction, then said, "Ann, I think you and your family will need to make sure each dog gets some individual attention over the next couple of weeks. Make sure you feed them separately, walk them separately, and this," she waved her arm at Nikka's barking and trying to chase Verona, "will get better. Just keep Verona on her leash for a few weeks."

She helped me attach Verona's tie-down cable to my side of the bed, went over some final instructions, made sure I had my take-home packet, and left.

The rest of the day, as long as I had Verona on her leash, Nikka was quiet and didn't approach us, except to sniff and get petted. Verona, bless her sweet soul, seemed to know that she was low dog and did her best to be calm and friendly. I know this helped Nikka adjust, but it still wasn't easy.

Editor's Note

Verklempt is a loan word from the Yiddish language that acts as an adjective. It has various alternative spellings. It means to be overwhelmed by emotion, perhaps so much that one cannot speak.

Where Is the Drill Sergeant When You Need One?

I not only worried about Nikka; I also grew anxious about Jerry and the kids spoiling Verona's training by not following along with what the school taught. I couldn't imagine what it would have been like if we hadn't already had a dog and known about brushing, feeding, walking routines, and other items of husbandry. I wished then, as well as now, that an instructor could magically appear at our door and say, "Okay, Family Chiappetta, listen up. I'm only here for the day, so get with it!"

The instructor, whom I will name Mr. Pip, and imagined as a combination of a drill sergeant and park ranger, complete with a whistle and Smokey the Bear hat, would whip my family into shape with a crash course in guide–dog etiquette, DOs and DON'Ts of service dog ownership, and how to walk with someone working a guide dog. Hmm. Maybe we did need a Marine drill sergeant for this, minus the expletives and Marine potty talk.

"Hey, you numbnuts," he would snap at Jerry, "what don't you understand about not feeding the dog people food?"

Or, "Left, left, left, dog on left," when my son or daughter walked her for me.

Wishful thinking, but I can dream, can't I?

Getting back to reality, and Nikka, two weeks later I had to call the school, because now Nikka was aggressively nipping Verona, and Verona was feeling harassed. Her body language was telling us that, and not wanting to let it go on any longer, I put in a call to the instructors' line.

I remember getting emotional when leaving the message. I recall thinking, What if this means we have to give up Nikka? What if this does damage to Verona?

So many doubts were roiling around in my head. Jerry was also worried, and he helped me keep Nikka from resorting to the chasing and nipping as often as he could. The kids did, too.

I knew it just couldn't continue but felt so helpless to stop it. Nikka was a rescue dog, and just thinking we would have to make a choice between keeping Verona and re–homing Nikka because I needed a guide dog made tears come to my eyes. I felt conflicted, so guilty and so frustrated that I couldn't get Nikka to understand how important she still was to me, how she had mended my broken heart. She was the one who helped us heal after we had to euthanize two dogs, Gunny and Rocky, in a year's time. She deserved our best, and I felt I was letting her down. What was worse, I felt like I was letting Verona down, too, and the thoughts of being "a bad blind person" returned.

I think Verona was relieved to get up and go to work with me back then, and I didn't blame her. Who wanted to feel unwanted?

A day later, an instructor returned my call. I explained what was going on, noting that we were afraid it wouldn't stop.

"You're doing all the right things," she said. "Remember to give equal time to both, especially you. Walk each and feed each separately. Two more weeks, if it doesn't get better, we'll come down to see what's up. Don't worry about Verona. She'll be okay as long as you keep up the bonding and stop the behavior when it starts."

She rang off, and I felt better just talking about it and knowing we weren't doing anything wrong or missing something. Four days later, it stopped. Nikka decided to accept Verona and began ignoring her. The relief was felt by the whole family.

The next family challenge—drum roll, please—was working the guide dog in the supermarket, in other stores, and in outdoor venues.

Traveling Together

I knew Verona and I had the skills to work out how to manage these situations. While at Guiding Eyes, we were told that the reason why training lasts 26 days is to instill all the skills for working safely as a team and to set us up for success. This was certainly true for the team, but how do we get our friends and family to go along with it when they really don't know how? It was one thing being with the instructors; they knew how to interact with the students and graduates. But what I was discovering was that most people don't know how to even greet us, let alone direct us or walk with us.

While you're in the guide dog school bubble, almost everyone you come into contact with knows just how to interact with a blind person and a guide dog team. There isn't any awkwardness. The serving staff and instructors anticipate your needs, like telling you which side your cup is placed on at lunch, or how to direct you in an understandable way. The facility is designed so a person who is blind or using what sight is left has little or no trouble navigating it. We are treated as people first.

I put my cane away the day I got there and didn't take it out again until I went back to work, keeping it as a backup.

Guiding Eyes has had decades of practice in making the in-residence student experience as worry-free as possible, so the student can bond with his or her dog and absorb as many of the instructions as possible. Even the coffee pod brewer was marked in braille. The stairs to the dining hall were high contrast, the hallways were lit to limit glare, and there was someone around to help all the time. By the second day you are at guide dog school, you begin to feel comfortable, and after 26 days of it, going home is a shock.

The weeks at the school are often the first time a person is exposed to a blind–centric program and campus where, possibly for the first time ever, a person doesn't feel like the exception, the one to pity, or feel anxiety about learning how to navigate in a dangerous or unfamiliar place. I felt like it was going back to college, like we were all in a sorority or some other sought–after program. I have heard over the years that this kind of strength–based treatment is often the last thing blind people expect, and at first it is hard to leave the cane in the corner or folded up in the suitcase.

It's also the reason why it feels like home.

Taking this one step further, now your family and friends have to absorb it, too, and without the caring and expert examples of the staff, it can be and was disappointing to me.

When I asked Jerry to walk behind me and to the right, he often complained that we were walking too slowly. My daughter told me it was annoying to have to do things differently just because of the new dog. Even now, over eight years later, I still wish for the magical guide dog school drill sergeant, Mr. Pip.

I wanted Mr. Pip to shadow us when Jerry or a coworker forgot to walk behind us and to the right. "Hey, meathead, what part of walking on the right of the handler don't you get? Your momma didn't raise a dummy, did she?"

I wanted Mr. Pip to insert his military chutzpah and block folks from petting my dog and say, "What part of no don't you understand?"

I wanted him to stride up to those pet parents who walked those little dogs on flexi leashes and say, "Get your puntable under control, you civvie. Can't you tell you are doing this guide dog team a disservice by letting Fluffy run up to them?"

In all honesty, real life isn't always like this. But more often than not, pedestrians text while they walk those sweet little pooches and are only aware of the approach of the zipline–like leash after I begin telling them it's a bad idea to let their dog try to greet my dog.

Okay, while we are on the subject of the non–initiated and why guide dogs do the things they do, I will admit that I get annoyed when I hear the following complaints:

Why can't the dog shoreline to the right? Answer: It's easier for the dog to follow the left line of travel and keep the handler away from obstacles. What I want to say: "Ya know, I don't care if it inconveniences people; I'm going with the dog. The folks who can see can get out of my way. My dog is working to keep me safe, not to be concerned about whether we follow the wall to the right or to the left."

Other comments are:

"Your dog looks sad in that thing."
"You mean the harness?"
"Yes. Isn't it heavy?"
"Not really."
"He still looks sad. Is that normal?"
"He's concentrating on being a good dog."
"Can I pet him?"
"No, he's working,"
"Oh, that's why he looks so sad."
Oh, here comes Mr. Pip to the rescue....

"Bark, woof, woof, woof." (This coming from a person, possibly in the supermarket, or on the street.)
Mr. Pip can give them a war face to help warn them away.

"What's your dog's name?"
"Buddy."
Person starts calling dog. Dog ignores them.

"Your dog is dumb. He doesn't even know his name."

Person makes kissing and smooching noises.
"Please don't distract my dog."
"I wasn't. I was just saying hello," person huffs.

And so on.

My son was good about it, though, perhaps because he had also been the better human guide in general. To be fair, April was young and Jerry was just being stubborn, and eventually it all did work out.

The general public isn't so accepting or informed. I don't mean to say that John and Jane Smith do unwise things on purpose, but being in public with a service or guide dog takes a bit of educating on both sides.

To help counteract the general public's ignorance about guide dogs, over the years, I have taken part in elementary school presentations. I believe that teaching children about people with disabilities when they're young helps them evolve into caring and empathetic adults. They will grow up to practice treating people with disabilities as people first and to expect and foster universal design, which is why I continue to take part in the presentations.

They're not always dry lectures, either. I've danced and sung with nursery school–aged children and performed for older kids, too. I love to connect with people and especially with kids. They are our future, and we are their mentors. I wish adults were just as easy to educate. I hope that if you read this book, you will also find it in your heart to help by correcting the uninformed so folks like me can go about our daily lives more easily.

Dynamic Duo

I was most comfortable working Verona alone or with another guide dog team. No offense to my crib, but the dog knows best. Verona was and still is a very smart dog. Back then, it took only one or at most three repetitions of a behavior or target or pattern for it to become part of her mental repertoire. She learned how to keep me lined up with the shopping cart and not bump me into it and when to pull us over even before Jerry would think to ask. She was wonderful following another person once I pointed them out and asked her to follow them.

One time, early in our partnership, Jerry and I went shopping at West Point. We went down an aisle in the commissary, and once we got to the end, he turned and said, "There was an entire sandwich lying on the floor, no wrapper, and Verona didn't even look at it. That's amazing."

I praised her, and I swear the look on her face was smug. I could hear her thinking, "What did you expect me to do? I'm working."

She was the consummate professional, but did give in to her dogginess once in a while.

The first time we took her to the Renaissance Fair, she dove for a turkey bone, potato skin, and empty bread bowl, all within the first 20 minutes. Remembering training, out came the dreaded head collar. I worked her in it for about 30 minutes, then took it off. After only one time, she never went after fair food again for the rest of her working career.

The fair was always fun, and many times things went awry. There were times I became impatient with Verona when in crowds. For instance, if we were walking against the crowd, she would just pull us over and stop. She would twitch her ears and shuffle as if to say, "Mom, you sure you want to go that way?" Once Jerry assured me there wasn't anything dangerous in our path, I'd pressure her forward and make her work against the wandering people. It was at times like that when I would wonder if Verona wasn't just a tad overcautious.

The funniest thing that happened at the Renaissance Fair wasn't so funny at the time, but looking back on it, I smile and laugh.

It had been a sloppy summer, rainy, and the fairground was muddy in places. I was in costume, which included a long skirt. Verona was following Jerry as he made his way to a booth, avoiding the muddy patches of ground.

Suddenly, she stopped, jerking me off balance. I tried to stop but ended up stumbling and going ankle deep in a mud puddle. I made a sound of disgust, grabbing my skirt to keep it from getting dirty, and at the same time realizing it was too late.

"God damn it," I snapped at Jerry, "why the hell did you take us this way?"

Jerry had gone ahead and didn't even know what had happened.

I was so mad, I flung away Verona's leash and harness handle and just stood there, fuming. Verona stood there, unmoving.

Jerry came back, looked at me, and said, "Verona stopped."

I wanted to throw a handful of mud at him just then. Cursing under my breath, I slogged my way out of the mud, my sandals and skirt ruined. We found a hose with running water, probably provided for just these kinds of incidents, and I washed off my feet and sandals until I could walk without squishing. I would have to wait until later to wash off the sandals and let the dry cleaner try to clean the skirt.

Later on, as I was scrubbing the mud from my sandals, Jerry said, "Honey, that really was funny. If you could have seen the look on your face…"

This wouldn't be the first time I overwalked Verona and hurt either my pride, or my body, or both. It also wasn't the first time I blamed Jerry when none of it was his fault.

In fact, at this point, I'd say that working a guide dog is physically demanding at times, and one has to get used to the risk of stumbling, falling, and feeling a bit foolish. I don't think it's any more or less risky than going out with a white cane; it's just different. I would have stepped in that mud puddle with a white cane, too. Maybe I would even have gotten stuck or fallen in all the way. Taking a chance and going out and being open to challenges is the key, and I think it's less intimidating with my dog leading the way.

As for the Renaissance Fair, the good memories with Verona are many and give me an inner warmth to which only a handler can attest. Each year, the Irish lady saw us and welcomed Ye Royale Canine and the Lady to the Queen's Fair. She would always make me smile. There was the time the vendor selling horns tried to fit a pink pair onto Verona's head. She just sat and let him do it. The man was so impressed, he let us have them for free.

These are the most powerful stories for me, and they rank right up there with memories of my wedding, the births of my children, and other milestones in my life.

Barricades

(The following essay was printed in a number of small press publications as well as on my blog. You can find that at www.thought-wheel.com.)

Verona and I follow the wide sidewalk in downtown White Plains. It is a route we traverse every workday. She puts on the brakes so hard I'm jerked to a full stop. "Whoa!" I say out loud, put out my foot, and feel some kind of construction barrier. My hand feels the yellow caution tape strung out above it.

I praise her and say, "Forward." She hesitates briefly, sizing up her options. Then she pulls me to the left and slowly eases us through a clear area between a large tree and the broken walkway. We skirt the barrier with careful steps, and when we're clear, I stop and praise her, rubbing her ears and letting her know just how much I appreciate her work. I imagine her satisfied look, as if to say, "I know, Mom. Don't worry. I won't let you down." After three years, I still get blown away by her ability to keep me safe, to make judgments and decisions that would otherwise have me at a serious disadvantage if I were out there with a white cane.

On the way back, with lunch in hand, we face the barrier again. This time, since the clearance is trickier going in the other direction, she takes me out into the street, parallel to the curb, and back onto the sidewalk when we are past the barrier.

I think to myself, as we go, I hope someone is watching. I

want to tell everyone how special she is, and I know that there are no true obstacles a dog and a person cannot overcome with perseverance, practice, and patience. I wish the other human interactions and challenges in life were as simple to solve.

For instance, sometimes days blur into one another and routines dull our senses. Fortunately, working a guide dog limits the dullness of repetition. Today is a good example of this. I wish I could take the lesson I learned of working past the barricade and apply it to some of the other concerns at issue in my life right now. I wish I could heal the problems facing me and those I love. Most of all, I want to share that feeling of complete trust and unconditional love and the solid bond felt between me and Verona and hand it over to those I am at odds with. I want to show them that if we allow it, we can work around and overcome barricades like misunderstandings and communication failures.

I want to tell them, What could be more important than working together to get past a hole in the ground?—that if we allow it, we can work around the roadblocks of life, just like a guide dog team.

Domiciliary Dynamics

One of the dynamics I found myself fascinated with during training was getting to know the other students. Our class was fairly small, only nine people, with one of them on the fast track for retraining after retiring his third dog. We came from all over the country, but I was the only local student, living only 40 minutes away from the main facility in Yorktown Heights, New York. There was a student from Washington State, one from Chicago, one from a suburb of Boston, and even another New York graduate from the Albany area, among others. I bonded with a young woman named Amanda, who was from Washington. She and I often sat together during meals. She was matched with a sweet Yellow Labrador named Renny who used to bark in her sleep and wake herself up, as if to say, "Who was *that?*"

One thing I liked about our group was how we got through the weather conditions. We laughed it off, mostly, and drank a lot of hot drinks. I realized that when I was feeling especially low or felt a lack of confidence, my fellow students were there to boost me up a little, share a caring word, or distract me and make me laugh with a corny joke.

I will always remember when Amanda crocheted each of us hats during the down time while waiting to practice our routes. I still have mine. I remember another funny time when the short-track student was sitting in the coffee room, and as I came in, his dog jumped into his lap. I burst out laughing. This was a large

Yellow Lab weighing about 75 pounds.

Verona's kennel mate, Sawyer, and his new handler, Eugene, were often my buddies during lunch. Sawyer and Verona would lie under the booth together like old friends, which they were after having been kenneled and trained together for four months. Verona also had three of her siblings in our class.

The acceptance of dogs and people was wonderful. Jolene was raising a Shepherd pup named Kisco. He liked to jump up and kiss your face when she wasn't looking. He was also present during lectures and often placed his paw on the lecture book whenever Jolene put it down on the floor to talk.

We passed the time a few nights by playing cards, listening to country music, and relaxing, our dogs lying quietly under the table in a dog huddle. We didn't just bond with our dogs, but also made friends with the other handlers, too.

The reason we trainees did our best to get along with everyone else was simple: We spent 12 hours a day together, sharing meals and lectures and sitting in the training lounge, waiting for our turn to walk our route with a new dog and trainer. It was much more tolerable to spend that time enjoying it instead of dreading it. I liked all my fellow classmates and wanted them to succeed as much as they wanted it for me. It was a mutually supportive group.

On a related note, up to only a year before the time I went into training, which was 2009, students had been required to share a dorm room. I cannot imagine sharing a room with another student I did not know, then having to adjust to a new dog, too. The students who had begun training in the early years were domiciled this way to give them a chance to get to know the other students. I'm glad I didn't have to do that. It would have interfered with my routine and bonding time with my dog.

As of this writing, most, if not all, in-residence guide dog training programs in the U.S. provide single rooms and amenities similar to or equal to a hotel or motel. Specifically, Guiding Eyes supplies students with a private room, bathroom, double-sized bed, nightstand, desk, chest-of-drawers, and adjustable heating and cooling unit. There is a vanity area adjacent to the closet. Each room has a refrigerator, TV, and Wi-Fi. There is a door that opens to the outside for relieving your dog independently. Students and staff can use the other sitting areas, and drinks and snacks are available 24/7. Students are expected to do laundry and confer with the on-duty nurse should the student have any ongoing medical needs. It is truly a home away from home.

During class, the student, or trainee, is provided with meals, amenities, and training so that he or she can learn to successfully work a dog. The less the student has to be distracted by or concerned about, the more he or she can absorb and practice the skills of teamwork.

Every time I go to visit the Guiding Eyes campus, it's like coming home again. I feel comfortable, my dog knows the surroundings, and best of all, I've made friends with and respect the organization for what they do.

Winter Woes

What I didn't expect during training were the sore muscles, the chapped skin, and the sand.

Let me explain. The first surprise was how different walking with a dog was from walking with a cane or just walking. One has to lead out with the left foot so the dog can more easily anticipate your actions. This means that while waiting at a curb, the right leg needs to become the stable leg. I soon had a very sore thigh from the muscles straining to keep that position over and over. Shin splints were another concern due to the faster and more demanding pace required to follow the new dog.

The elements kept my hands and feet cold, and the windburn on my face was amusing to Jerry, what he calls raccoon face. Also, my legs were wind–burned where my coat and socks ended.

I mentioned sand. It's the only chemical–free and safe ground treatment for traction on ice and snow for dogs. Unfortunately, it gets tracked in and infiltrates every nook and cranny, including beds. The only other time I had more sand in my bed was in Aruba. I took to wearing slippers and brushing out my bed before turning in for the night. The cleaning staff at Guiding Eyes swept every day, but still we all found sand in our shoes and laundry baskets and between the sheets.

Each class was headed by a supervisor and team of instructors aided by an instructor's assistant, or IA. Our supervisor was Dell Rodman. He didn't 'fess up to the ice cream store incident until years afterward, when I was in class training with my second dog, Bailey. While I was in class, I found Dell to be a kind and knowledgeable person. He truly loves dogs and is passionate about working and training them. I was also fortunate to spend some time with Dell and other Guiding Eyes training staff during national blindness conventions. He met my family, and I realized that he and my husband had the same bent sense of humor.

Dell got me a second time a few years after I was matched with Verona. I was waiting to cross the street in downtown White Plains, the same area where Guiding Eyes trained both dogs and the new teams. I was only five blocks from the training lounge and sometimes ran into instructors and other students.

One always knew when there was another team approaching. The dog's head would rise up and the pace would quicken, the excitement transferred through the harness and leash. Then I would hear the handler or the instructor talking, plus the jingle of tags, and we would pass while saying, "Leave it!" and "Hup up!" Or the instructor would say, "New team coming up on your right," and I would know to keep my dog from veering toward them.

This time, I was the unsuspecting victim of Dell's sense of humor. I stood at the corner, waiting for the light to change and for the audible signal to begin beeping. A man appeared behind me and asked, "Excuse me, do you need help crossing the street?"

"No, thanks. We're good."

"How do you do that?"

I turned toward him, ready to give him a polite but firm brushoff.

"Ann, it's Dell," he said, and I burst out laughing.

"Do you always stand at street corners and harass the blind people?" I asked, a teasing tone in my voice.

This time he laughed. We exchanged some news, and then continued to our intended destinations.

It was always gratifying to run into other guide dog teams and instructors from Guiding Eyes or other schools. It gave me a sense of belonging, that, up until a few years prior to being matched with a dog, I had struggled with most of the time.

Strength in Numbers

Disability is often isolating and lonely. Before I began participating in groups made up of others like myself, I really was missing out. Once I began socializing with other blind folks, a whole new world opened. I began making new friends and learning new things and felt I wasn't so alone anymore.

The first time I traveled with a small group, accompanying other blind people, I discovered how much I had missed traveling and having fun. The challenges of travel were frustrating at times; however, even my sighted friends found it so, and this knowledge grounded me. Heck, if my sighted friends got frustrated, lost, and such when navigating an airport or train station, I was in good company, right? It wasn't so different for me after all, and this gave me hope. I learned my limits and when to ask for help. I learned how to effectively communicate my needs, which was one of the hardest skills to accomplish, mostly because I had to learn how to be vulnerable and admit when I was unable to do something myself.

I also challenged myself from time to time, taking on a task I found a little bit intimidating. I learned to become more self–reliant through volunteering in various roles in the American Council of the Blind, or ACB. I started going to local chapter meetings, then progressed until I found myself chairing committees on the national level for the special interest group Guide Dog Users, Inc., or GDUI. Although I have since ended my active participation in GDUI and have passed on the leadership role to other members, those who are younger, I dedicated five years of my time on the board of directors and was able to learn how to be a better advocate for the blind while serving as a board member.

Saying Goodbye

It is very difficult to mourn the progressive loss of vision over a long period. When speaking with other individuals who are just beginning to experience retinal degeneration, I often find myself becoming sad, recalling the early years and how depressing it was for me. I have come to realize that remaining in a constant state of waiting for the next piece of my vision to end was, and still is, just about impossible to cope with in a positive manner. Every time there's a drop in visual field and the increase of other symptoms, there are emotions and feelings one must also face. For me, the anxiety of becoming more dependent upon others and feeling useless led to depression and more anxiety. I was also afraid of not being able to continue to do the things I loved, like enjoying the beauty of nature, art, and other visually stimulating activities.

Below is an essay written and published in the Winter 2014 issue of DIALOGUE Magazine.

"What I Want to Remember"

I lost my sight at the age of 28 and resigned from my job because of it. I worked as a designer for an acrylic furniture company and could no longer perform my job duties, which were all visual in nature. I mourned this part of my life more than any other because I didn't know how to take all the creative energy and transfer it into something else. One night, out of sheer frustration, I began to write. First it was poetry, most of it fanciful and meaningless. This turned into journaling and short stories, which led to some successful small press literary magazines publishing my work. It wasn't until much later, when I was in college, that I realized I'd made the transition from expressing myself with the visual arts to those of the literary kind. From this point, I resolved to develop my talent because I knew it would become an essential part of learning how to successfully live with a disability.

What I didn't realize back then was that retraining my mind was the cornerstone of the transition into blindness. I will always remember what life was like before it, and I am grateful that I do have the visual references of the first 26 years of my life to help me go forward.

Images have a way of tattooing themselves onto the psyche. If they are referenced enough, one will never forget them. All writers use this sensory recall as an essential tool to enhance the craft. What I didn't know at the time was that developing it would one day help me deal with losing my sight.

I call this my soul sense, and it incorporates personal visual experiences with other sensory skills, like touch, sound, smell, and taste.

For instance, when I hear a jet plane, my mind cues up the image; when someone points out a beautiful sunset, I recall one. I use the power of observation to keep the memories close; that way, I will never be without a reference.

Of course, there will be surprises, like when I expected the nappa leather bag to be black or brown, and the sales clerk told me it was electric blue. I'd never seen electric blue leather bags, so it took me a moment to put the image and the color together in my mind.

Blindness is a way of being, a distinct circumstance in which a person learns how to navigate through life. To ignore it means we are ignoring ourselves and denying the personal growth to cope with the emotional nature of living without it.

Retinal degeneration has made my world monochromatic. I do, however, remember the colors I can no longer detect. In my mind's eye, the flat gray and black bushes dotted with stark white blobs are blooming forsythias lining the sidewalk. The vivid yellow flowers and light green leaves under the blue sky are only memories.

Does this sadden me? Frustrate me? It used to, but not now. It happened so gradually that I had time to adjust. I already knew what forsythia looked like, so for me, even when the color blindness began, the reference guide in my head kept me from feeling like I was missing out on something.

Retinal degeneration has also rendered me night blind. Beginning when I was about 10 years old, the lack of any form of light filled me with anxiety. It made me feel so helpless. Now, however, I do my best to face the dark with courage, though I don't always succeed.

If I could impress just one piece of advice upon a young visually impaired person, I would tell them to never give up, learn braille and mobility skills, and trust themselves to know when to ask for help. I would ask this young person to remember the golden rule of true independence: Know when and how to ask others for help to achieve it. We are, after all, interdependent. Learning how and when to ask for assistance will open doors and prevent social isolation.

What I miss seeing the most: the faces of those I love. What I don't miss: the ugliness of suffering and violence.

What advice do I have for someone who is progressing into blindness? Do your best to let your mind file away what you want to remember visually.

If you've seen a breathtaking view of the Grand Canyon, even if it was only a photo, when you are actually standing at the rim, it won't really matter. You will be smelling, tasting, and listening to the majesty of that wondrous place. Your soul sense will aid in the expansion and creation of new memories.

Ask yourself what you want to remember and make it happen.

Explore, ask questions, and refine your skills for those times you will need them most.

Making Progress with
This Thing Called Blindness

It's been 27 years since I first heard my diagnosis, and it has taken most of that time to accept and adjust to each declining stage of vision loss. The sadness, anger, and fear have all taken a toll on me. It would be Pollyannaish of me not to acknowledge it.

I suppose that the constant pressure to cope with loss molds a person in ways that others can misunderstand or misconstrue. I think, being realistic, that seeking hope in places where none can be found is pointless. Looking for hope and purpose and expressing the concepts creatively is one way I cope with loss. I pursue things that result in pleasurable and positive outcomes. I reject individuals or situations that do nothing to contribute to my happiness and purpose. Some folks have said I am a bit aloof and maybe even a tad arrogant. When I hear these comments, I just smile. Nothing could be further from the truth. If these folks could look into my heart, they would not find arrogance, just caution. What they think is aloofness is actually respect for the opinions and beliefs of others.

While I'm on the subject of perceptions, some people I know are frank enough to tell me they feel horrified when I say I'm ready to take the final plunge into blindness. They don't understand how tired I am of living with a hope that hasn't ever become a reality. Being able to see again is not my priority; sight–saving techniques cannot be administered. I think I began to mourn the loss when I was told to put on my first pair of glasses, my young mind realizing just how visually impaired I really was, and either instinct or intuition let me know this wasn't going to improve.

Acceptance is a long, hard road, as evidenced by the above essay and the post–2000 publishing year. It really did take over a decade for me to learn to cope with gradual vision loss. I've walked that road for a long time, felt the disappointments, the hurt, and the paralyzing fear, and yet I refused to allow myself to live indefinitely in the sadness and anger these feelings produced. I believed there was a way to cope, a way to understand and work around the limitations, and over time I found it. I found the answers—sometimes independently, and other times with help.

There were also many times when I had to accept the circumstances and walk away as a means of coping. These were the toughest lessons. For example, my memories of the times I tried to communicate with various schools can still trigger flares of anger. One of my child's administrators told me that because I couldn't see what was happening, I was perceiving things wrong. From that point on, I brought along my husband, whose support of my ability proved to the administrators that my child's education did not depend on my having vision. Another time, during my second year of undergraduate school, a clergyperson and administrator refused to give permission to provide the college's IT network with the software program that would help me access the network and campus computer and participate alongside the other students. I found another way to complete my assignments by asking the instructors to help me bypass this resistance.

There were many instances like this over the years, and it often left me feeling angry and frustrated and feeling as if I was the only one to be treated like a second–class citizen.

One of the situations, one that still brings me to tears,

happened while participating at back-to-school night when my son, Anthony, was still in high school. Verona and I had been a team for about four years. We were going down the staircase in front of the other parents and students. As we proceeded down the last two steps to the landing, we were shoved hard, and both Verona and I stumbled down the last two steps, almost falling. I grabbed the handrail and let go of her handle, and we were both able to keep our footing. I was so angry. I turned to the person behind me, not even knowing who it was, and said, "What the hell is your problem? Can't you see I'm using a guide dog? You almost made us fall, you idiot!"

The person pushed past, not even acknowledging us. I began to cry and had to pull over into the hallway to get hold of my emotions.

My children, behind me in the crowd, ran to me and asked what had happened, only able to see that I'd stumbled and almost fallen. While I was telling them what had happened, the school social worker came to me, asking what had happened, and my kids both said, "She was pushed."

He seemed skeptical and asked, "Did you see who it was?"

"I'm blind! What do you think?" I snapped, anger in my tone.

He did not even try to find out who it was and made an excuse to move on. I cried harder then, unable to hold back. My kids just stood there, waiting for me to stop. I hated showing them my vulnerability, this human weakness in someone who was supposed to be a role model. I was a victim of another's mean and ugly actions and lack of awareness—and worse, it went unacknowledged.

Sometimes when things like this happened, it was all I could do to manage my own reactions and hope my kids could understand. Other times, I refused to back down and would not be intimidated. This could be viewed as a character flaw at times and a boon at the times when standing up for something is the right thing to do.

I have learned to go on finding another way when faced with a barrier, whether it is an attitude or something physical. Finding the path of least resistance is often infuriating to those who block you, but if you're willing to continue and are ready to risk not getting a positive outcome for yourself and others, it should be done.

For a time, I encountered resistance from others when I said I wanted to apply for a guide dog. This fed my own doubts about not being a good enough blind person. One person actually said to me that I was being selfish because I could still see a little, and the dog I would get would be taken away from someone who had no vision at all. Talk about guilt! How could I fill out an application, knowing this? Thankfully, the mobility instructor who informed me I was blind enough got me out of that kind of thinking.

Back in the Saddle

I returned home with Verona in late January 2009, and the following Monday, I boarded the Paratransit bus and went back to work.

At the time, I was employed 30 hours a week as a youth group coordinator for an independent living center called Westchester Disabled on the Move, Inc. I developed and organized a strength–based program for high school–aged youth with emotional and developmental disabilities. It was my first real job after losing my vision in 1993. I'd obtained a master's degree in family therapy but couldn't find a job and took this position to tide me over until I could find something in my field of study.

Fortunately for me, there were already two other guide dog users in our office, so I really didn't have to do much educating. Verona was housed under my cubicle on a tie–down and padded bed. It wasn't much of an adjustment for either of us. The boys in my youth group back then loved her and learned to restrain themselves, all great learning tools for managing their impulsivity. Verona became the reward after we finished our group work. I would let her go and she would go visiting, greeting each of them. She was, and still is, gentle and attentive—and, I am told, has humanlike eyes that make people feel safe.

This is how Verona and I began our unofficial therapy work together, too. I never forced her to do it, didn't even know she was doing it, until we began working in nursing homes. Her ability to know which individuals needed to pet her and interact with her was uncanny.

One time, she poked her head under a curtain while I was visiting a cousin in the hospital. I started to apologize, and then came a giggle, and the man began petting her head, cooing in Spanish. Later, he told me in English that he loved dogs and was so happy that she'd let him pet her. I often took Verona to a children's hospital and let her pick out whom she wanted to spend time with. This often left me with tears in my eyes, knowing she had lifted the pain and fear or loneliness for just a little while.

I soon learned to appreciate that Verona was a very empathic dog. She would sit beside a client who was anxious, or place her head in the lap of a child in a wheelchair, or lie quietly at a client's feet to be petted. This was all pet–assisted therapy. Little by little, Verona's judgment became more and more on target. Each time she interacted with a client, I found it helpful overall. Eventually, I would learn to encourage her and prompt a client to pet her, and this led to some very powerful conversations and promoted healing and gaining a client's trust.

One time, while we were volunteering at a local children's hospital, Verona seemed very interested in a teen who was suffering from Friedreich's ataxia; this causes progressive damage to the nervous system. She kept sniffing his wheelchair wheels, and he smiled whenever she sat beside him. His chair, though, was so high that he couldn't reach down to pet her. I removed her harness and asked the staff to get two sturdy chairs. They placed them facing one another next to the wheelchair. I then asked Verona to jump onto the chairs and lie down across them. The teen, Jared, petted her for a long time, and she propped her head on his chair, letting him fondle her ears. He kept saying, '"She's beautiful. She's like velvet." The staff told me he smiled the entire time. Later, when I was leaving, the social worker who was with us told me that Jared rarely smiled or tried to use his arms or hands, and to watch him reach out to pet Verona gave her hope that pet–assisted therapy would help. To bear witness to someone like Jared finding peace while doing something as simple as petting a dog amazes me. Verona opened up a whole new way of appreciating new places and the people around me.

As a testament to this, below is an essay I wrote on our first family trip after getting Verona. Jerry, April, my mother–in–law (Carol), and I, along with Verona, drove to Ontario. This essay describes the experience.

Mist and Maple Leaves

(Originally printed in DIALOGUE Magazine; see below for full attribution.)

August 17–24, 2009

We're on the bridge poised between the flagpoles separating the United States and Canada.

"Hey, Mom, we're in two countries at once," says my daughter.

I don't think crossing into Mexico would feel the same. For one thing, we're surrounded by water, not desert. The Canadian border patrol officer is brisk and efficient, dismissing us once he inspects our papers. I don't think it would be this simple in Mexico.

In 15 minutes, we're over the bridge and heading to our hotel overlooking the falls.

The hotel lobby is busy and full of obstacles, and my guide dog expertly whisks me around them all and into the elevator. Luckily, our room is at the end of the hall and easy for me to find.

My daughter, husband, and mother–in–law ooh and aah over the view from the 36th floor facing the falls.

"It's beautiful, Mom," my daughter says.

I look out the window and realize that it's all lost to me. For her sake, I try to smile. I manage a horrible–sounding sigh instead.

"I wish I could see it." My words are choked, and I fight back tears. The hope of being able to sear the visual loveliness of Niagara Falls past my damaged eyes and into my memory flies away with the mist. For a few minutes, I'm overcome with grief. What a bittersweet way to take the final plunge into blindness, facing the daunting and unforgiving power of Niagara.

My guide dog, Verona, steps up to the glass and takes a look. I can tell by the way she holds her ears that she is thinking. It's at a time like this that I would willingly give away the rest of my sight to know what's going on inside her doggie brain. I stand beside her, knowing that she will make my time here less stressful. I can't wait to work with her while we tour Niagara and downtown Ontario.

Rather than obsessing about what I can't experience visually, I unpack. The busywork is calming. When I'm done, the grief is gone, replaced by anticipation of the pleasant sort mixed with resolve. I came here to learn how to vacation with my new guide dog and prove to myself and to family that I don't need my vision to do it. I just hope I didn't set the bar too high.

Our suite is spacious and well–appointed, a whirlpool tub and fireplace completing the amenities. Verona loves the plush, sculpted carpeting and inspects every inch at her leisure.

On day three, we take the deluxe bus tour, ending with the ride beside the falls on the Maid of the Mist. But first we are driven to other key points in and around the Lake District. Verona and I get the front seat behind the driver. The tour bus driver, Dave, is like a cross between a big brother and a walking history book. As we drive through the Niagara region, Dave tells us that the parkland and the falls are leased for tourism and maintained by the parks department. The Canadian government has control of the entire area. Even the casinos are leased out, he says, adding that the hotels and tourism by the falls have developed due to the government finally legalizing gambling.

During the tour, Verona has to work hard to keep me safe.

In one park, she is asked to keep up with our group. As the crowd parts to surge around a low stone bench, she stops short, but I keep moving and hit my knee against it. Before I can even react, my husband is urging us around it.

"Hurry up, or we'll lose our group."

We catch up, and when I finally feel my knee, I find a scrape, and it's already hot and swollen. I pop two ibuprofen tablets and choose to ignore the pain.

On our way back to the bus, I go past the bench and Verona guides me around it. I'm not quite sure what happened on our way in, but our little error makes her pay even closer attention now. I relax my doubt that she can keep me safe and remind myself that new teams will have moments like this. Our instructor at guide dog school was always reminding us to trust our dog. She also reminded us that younger dogs will make mistakes, and we need to pay attention to avoid potential errors. Perhaps if I'd paid closer attention to what Verona was trying to tell me, I wouldn't have overstepped her and hit my knee.

It's 2 p.m. when we finally get on line to board the boat for the falls. We're herded cattle–style into a small plaza outside the quay. It's hot, and I'm shoulder to shoulder with the other tourists. Verona stands with me, patient and stoic.

It takes an hour for us to finally get on the boat, and I don the blue plastic poncho; the hood barely covers my head, but it fits easily over my bag and body. The boat is shaped like a small ferry. The ride to the falls is only three minutes, and I hear the roar and feel the wind rushing under my thin plastic poncho. We ride along the horseshoe curve of the falls, and it is awesome; we're pelted with water and wind gusts so strong that our ponchos are being ripped off as we try to stuff them back in place. I'm yelling, laughing, and loving the feeling of the water and wind on my face and body. For a few moments, I forget I'm holding onto Verona's leash, and a stab of concern pulls me from my adrenaline rush. I look down, feeling her huddled under our legs, trying to avoid the water. I pet her and tell her it's okay. I get the feeling that she can't wait until it's over.

Then, as fast as it begins, it is over and we're back at the quay—wet, excited, and glad to have done it. I have just enough time on the way out to let Verona shake off the water, and I praise her as I dry her off.

That evening, we order pizza and have it delivered to our room. We're all wiped out from the tour, and even Verona takes a long nap on the king–sized bed, belly–up, her snores making me smile. It sounds so satisfying and less annoying coming from her than coming from my husband. Before long, I'm lulled to sleep by her soft sounds, footsore and ready to take on whatever comes our way.

* * * * *

There were, of course, many more experiences while tripping around Ontario. The takeaway was, for me, at least, that I could still enjoy myself.

Editor's Notes

"Mist and Maple Leaves" was published in the Spring 2010 issue of DIALOGUE Magazine. Copyright 2010 by Blindskills Inc., all rights reserved. Reprinted here with permission.
Website: www.blindskills.org

Online, there is much information about the Maid of the Mist boat tours at Niagara Falls, including this 12.5–minute YouTube video, uploaded by Hoosier Tim's Travel Videos.
https://www.youtube.com/watch?v=CLyurlxlG7Y

Home Away from Home

During the time beginning shortly after Verona and I became a guide dog team, I became good friends with the Guiding Eyes Manager of Consumer Services and Graduate Support, Becky Davidson. She introduced me to other guide dog users in the New York metro area and Hudson Valley. I began a lifelong connection with the guide dog lifestyle, and Becky helped me with making these connections. In fact, I've kept many of my guide dog friendships—not just with other handlers, but also with staff, mostly the training staff. This is natural, as over the years of volunteering and assisting Guiding Eyes, it becomes a part of one's identity.

Not all graduates feel this way, and this is also part of the natural course of things when leaving a training program. One leaves with the skills and the dog and reenters his or her life. Sometimes this means staying in touch; sometimes it doesn't. Either way, schools are flexible about it and can generally be reliable about follow–ups and other issues, should they occur. I thought of it as making a choice between being an active alumna or not. Some people decide to do something to give back in a more determined manner, which is also acceptable.

About 15 years ago, Guiding Eyes established a Graduate Council for those who want to give back and help with keeping communication with the general graduate population open. The council members assist with exit interviews and other information–gathering tasks. The thought was that if another graduate were at the end of the phone line, graduates would feel more relaxed and would be more likely to share constructive criticism, compliments, and other suggestions about the school and other amenities during training. Since its inception, the GC, as it is called, has been extremely successful.

The GC was also instrumental in advancing Guiding Eyes into hosting a continuing education seminar, or CES, which took place in April 2017. Over 75 guide dog teams and 80 puppy raisers and instructors and staff attended the weekend–long event. It was a powerful and purposeful event and made the commitment of supporting both the guide dog lifestyle and raising puppies to become guide dogs even more significant. It was the first of its kind, and it would not have been possible without the passion of the GC, puppy raisers, volunteers, and key staff members of Guiding Eyes.

Incidentally, I served on this graduate council for three years, ending my term as president in 2014. This opportunity, along with others like it, groomed me for the leadership roles I would take on later. I never thought of myself as a leader. I always thought of myself as a bit introverted and liking my solitude, but fate has a way of challenging one's views when undertaking such a life–changing responsibility as choosing to work with a guide dog.

What are some of these responsibilities?

The obvious ones are how to work and care for one's new partner. Learning the dog's biology and the best way to groom and reinforce obedience are the most important.

Staying consistent when working your dog is another important factor. That's why training with a new dog the first time is three or four weeks long at most schools. One must adopt the vocal intonations and body language associated with the dog's training. Hand signals, voice commands, and other gestures are repeated until they are second nature. Leash checks, harness checks, humane corrections, and judging when to re–work an error are most of the skills learned while working your dog in class. The instructor is behind you on the right, watching everything. I will always feel like they are guardian angels.

I recall one major flub I made during the second week of class. We were entering a mall. It was clear and cold, and the glare off the ice and snow was giving me pain; my eyes, even with the dark glasses, were already bothering me. I got out of the van and asked Verona to find the door. We were warned that if a row of doors was being offered, we had to do our best to keep the dog focused on only one door. We did this by repeating, "To the door" and not turning our shoulders away from the direction of the specific door. Verona found the door; I swept my hand across its surface until I found the handle, opened it, and we walked into the mall. As we walked into the darker ambience, vertigo gripped me and I panicked, stumbling into a Wet Floor sign.

Later, when Dell told me what had happened, I finally fully understood the severity of my condition and realized that someone else finally understood how it affected me. Until then, however, it was something I avoided talking about because I didn't know exactly what was happening. Just as on the night walk, I was at first very anxious that I'd made such an error, then was thankful that I'd done it in front of the instructors, who would help me find positive ways to deal with it.

Dell approached me after I found a seat near the coffee shop. "What happened?" he asked, sitting next to me.

"I don't know," I shrugged. I was feeling like a bumbling blinkie just then and may have been mumbling.

"It looked like you lost your balance a little," he said.

I thought about it, then nodded, trying not to let the

frustration I was holding inside make the tears spill out. I swallowed, took a deep breath, then said, "Yes, maybe I did."

"Do you have trouble going from bright light to dark places?" he asked.

"Yes." This may have been more like a croak and a nod.

"Okay. So, from now on, when you know you are going from light to dark or from dark to light, give yourself time to adjust. It's okay to stop, to count to 10, then go. Don't worry about who's behind you. You concentrate on you and your dog, okay?

I nodded, not being able to make the lump in my throat subside enough to speak. Dell waited for me to speak.

I took another deep breath, then was finally able to say something. "Okay, I'll do that." I found my voice again and added, "It wasn't Verona's fault that we knocked down the Wet Floor sign."

Dell may have been smiling. "It happens. It's okay," he said, patting my shoulder. "Just give yourself time to adjust when going from one extreme to the other. Just think about you and your dog."

It was the first time someone validated my struggles and gave me permission to do whatever I needed to in order to accommodate my disability. It empowered me, gave me more confidence, and provided me with a strategy that has assisted me since that day.

More Than Just a Dog

Many graduates volunteer to speak at fundraisers and other events. I've met puppy raisers and folks who have adopted a dog that was released from the training program to become a family pet. One of my sisters has a Guiding Eyes release dog. I've met law enforcement officers who, upon seeing us, give my dog a once-over, then say, "Isn't that a Guiding Eyes dog? He looks just like our narcotics dog."

It is a testament to the human and canine bond to hear a police officer become verklempt as he recounts having to put down his canine partner after 9, 11, or 14 years. Some of them don't ever get another dog, for obvious reasons. The loss of a partner is just too great to risk losing another best friend.

I asked a long-time guide dog handler how she could retire a dog for a younger one. She answered me with honesty that I didn't understand then but appreciate now. She told me that the best part of being a guide dog handler is being able to love and bond with each dog, one at a time. She also said it hurt every time she retired a dog or lost a dog to death or illness, but she feels like a very lucky person to have had the opportunity to be part of the dog's life and to have given the dog a purpose and a safe and happy place to be.

As Verona and I grew as a team, there were many firsts, not just going on vacation and riding the Maid of the Mist in Niagara Falls. We attended seminars, took part in outdoor events and activities, and went to nursing homes and schools. She got to sit in a Blackhawk helicopter and an Army Jeep, guided me through the tunnel of lights in the Ripley Museum, and camped with us many times.

The only first I wish we had not accomplished together, although it ended up being comforting, was attending wakes, memorials, and funerals.

The first was the wake for my godmother. Verona took me to the kneeler and, at a word, lay quietly until I had paid my respects. The last service we attended together as a working team was for a veteran who had died. When he attended his therapy sessions, Verona sat between his legs, and he would stroke her head while talking. Eventually she would lie down and roll onto her back, and he would rub her belly, too.

As we stood on the hill overlooking his burial ceremony, I wondered if Verona understood what was happening. She was on her best behavior, standing with me while my colleague described what was taking place. We listened to the priest as he recited the burial prayer, and we returned to the car after the last note of Taps faded out and the color guard handed the folded flag to his mother. It was my dog who comforted me the most during times like that, and I am sure I am not speaking only for myself when I say that sometimes my dog comforts me in a way a person simply cannot.

Before I was matched with Verona in 2009, I would not have attempted half of the activities that I did after she came into my life. Nor would I have traveled nearly as often, given that I would have had to depend on a human guide to take me through everything. Some folks might say, "Well, isn't that better? More reliable?" I will say only this: A human guide assumes a lot of the control; a guide dog doesn't. A human partner pulls you along, often making you feel like the proverbial rolling luggage, while a guide dog understands the teamwork required. This keeps the balance and lets the handler assume more control than if he or she were being led by a human guide.

I know there is going to be some pushback against what I am stating here on these pages, but think about it: Vision loss sucks. Living with it means having to give up an inordinate amount of control and decision-making and allowing others to take over. If a guide dog could give back that sense of independence, wouldn't that be rewarding?

People aren't always ready to help, either. Unless one has a personal attendant, which most don't, the limitations are overwhelming. I prefer to think of it this way: The best thing would be for people to guide people, but society and culture cannot carry the responsibility like a loyal, always-ready companion the way a guide dog does. Being aware of this human shortcoming, we have instead trained dogs to be our true companions, our ready and reliable way to travel the path of independence.

Below is a blog post written after I was a guest at a transition meeting for Guiding Eyes. On occasion, I have stayed and met with the graduates who were returning for their successor dogs.

* * * * *

Verona and I walk into the dining room, where the new students are already sitting down for dinner. It is dog day tomorrow. It's hard to believe it's been almost three years since it was dog day for me. Verona finds an empty seat. I settle her under the table and then ask what's on the menu.

"Pork tenderloin, roasted potatoes, and sautéed green beans," replies the server, "and help yourself to the garlic bread while it's still hot."

It's good to be back, I think, reaching for the bread basket. Between bites of warm, crusty bread, I introduce myself to the other folks at the table. The night before dog day is probably the most important and nerve–racking day for each person in the room tonight. It is especially complex for the men and women who are returning to be matched with a successor dog. New students don't normally carry the emotions and feelings of loss associated with retiring a dog; to help the students move on, most guide dog schools offer counseling as part of the adjustment process.

"I'm here to talk to all the retrains tonight," I say.

During dinner I discover that three women I'm sitting with are retrains: one coming back for her fourth dog, and the other two moving on to a second. Moving on from dog one to dog two is a particularly difficult shift for a guide or service dog handler, because the first dog symbolizes an extraordinary change in the handler's life. The increased sense of confidence and independence the first dog provides is a powerful catalyst and bonds the handler and dog so strongly that it is difficult for the handler to move on to a successor dog.

After dinner and the lecture, I gather up four retrains and we settle into the student living room to begin the group meeting.

The woman who is there for her fourth dog says, "I really don't think I need to come. I'm used to it."

I lead the other three students upstairs, and we each find seats. As we begin talking, another student joins us, a man.

"I feel so guilty," confides the first woman, speaking about her dog. "I'm so afraid she doesn't understand. I want her to be happy, but she still tries to work even when she can't walk." She starts to cry.

"I know," says the second woman. "It breaks my heart to walk out of the house without her, but she can't do it anymore. She lies down after walking a block or two."

The third woman says, "It's been hard, but in a way I'm okay with it because she's staying with us, and I don't have to say goodbye."

All three women are keeping the first dog—which, incidentally, often eases the anxiety leading up to the retirement of the first dog. Some handlers, however, do return the dog to the puppy raiser or hand them over to a family member or friend. Many guide dog users cannot care for more than one dog at a time, and for those folks, the transition is much more troubling.

"I had to give up my dog three years ago because of my own health problems," says the man. "I tried keeping in touch with his puppy raisers, but one day I told them to stop. I couldn't take it anymore. Doesn't that sound so selfish?"

"It sounds like you had to do it so you could get better," I say. "That isn't selfish."

He nods. "Yes, but I miss him. I feel like I let him down. I hope a new dog will help me feel better about it."

By the end of our talk, all four students were sharing stories, and all reported to me before we left that they were glad they had joined the group.

As Verona and I left the room, it felt gratifying knowing we had helped ease some of the pain of letting go. The last thought I had before bed that night was that I was happy that each one of the students was going to open their heart to a new beginning inspired by four healing paws and a harness.

Moving On

(Written in 2012)

I've had to grow into the role of guide dog handler, just like I grew into the role of being a blind person, counselor, wife, and mom. Even the glorified hobby of writing was a growth process, so it was no surprise when one day I realized that Verona and I were now a mature, synchronized team. It's taken just about three years from the time I entered guide dog school and fumbled my way through it to achieve this goal. Looking back, it was worth every hour, every sore muscle, and all the emotional challenges to earn it. What's more, it helped my family cope better with my blindness, too.

For instance, there was always the pre–traveling anxiety: who would guide me, could I do it myself, and so on and so forth. Once we figured out how to work together, it was manageable. My cane was always with me, and I did my best to use it, but it seemed that whenever we were out, the crowds were nearly impassible and I always resorted to a sighted guide.

This all changed when I came home with Verona. There are still times when I take an arm and heel her, but those times are the exception, now, not the rule. She navigates crowds and guides me safely up and down stairs and through traffic, so I can keep up with my friends and family when we're together. I'm no longer a burden to them, and it's a blessing to know I can be more independent so we can all have more fun.

Then there is the night and the anxiety it provokes. Retinal degeneration is a wicked disease. It is incurable, and the symptoms are different from person to person. As I progress further into my particular stage of night blindness symptoms, it's been hard to go out at night. The dark presents me with a form of vertigo that I cannot easily overcome. I do my best to not allow it to limit me, but it does. Traveling in the dark makes me feel vulnerable and helpless, and I hate it. I can sometimes work through the dizziness and disorientation, but it's hard unless I have Verona guiding me. Trusting her is the only way I can work through this fear and not become overly dependent upon others.

My fear of the dark goes back to when I was a child. I thought everyone else was just like me and couldn't see in the dark. I fell over or ran into things, always hurting myself, and unless it was severe, I hid it from others. It wasn't until I was 17 and got lost in the woods during a camping trip that I realized I was completely night blind. I could barely see a flashlight beam. It was the worst shock for me to admit I would never be normal.

Then came the night walk at guide dog school. I was terrified, but I hid it until the instructor told me I was too quiet and tense, and if I wanted Verona to work well for me, I had to trust her and relax.

"Follow your dog," she said. "If you get dizzy, just stop and take deep breaths until it passes."

That night, I learned two things: that I really did trust Verona, and that when I was tense, it made her tense and could interfere with our progress, even for a mid-paced walker like me.

So, I'm no night owl, and for safety's sake, I only go out at night with Verona, who has flashing lights attached to her harness. I still get a little nervous, but every time we go out and come back safe, it boosts me up for the next time. There are going to be times when I have to do it all on my own, without sighted assistance, and I hope all those times, my dog is leading the way.

Part Three

Making the Transition

The Paratransit van pulled up to my friend's house and stopped, the beep indicating that the driver had put it in Park.

It was a horrible night, a summer storm whipping up just before we were ready to finish up our monthly Westchester Council of the Blind meeting. Another friend, who also worked a female Black Lab, and Verona and I boarded the van and buckled up.

The sound of thunder shook the van. Then the crack of lightning followed. Verona's nose nudged my hand, and I felt her trembling, which troubled me. My friend's Lab was lying quietly, but my dog was visibly stressed. I took out a few treats and gently asked her to settle, then fed her a few while we drove through the storm. Eventually she calmed, but I knew something was wrong. She had her seventh birthday coming up in November, and I was worried. I spoke about it to my friend, and she did her best to reassure me that this was just a really bad storm, and any dog, even the best, could have a bad day. So I let it pass.

A few months later, Verona began slowing down. My other friends with guide dogs and my family noticed. I was almost always the last team to make it across a street or parking lot, and it was not too long after these pacing issues that I knew Verona was telling me she wanted to retire. She was healthy, active, and still wanted to go places, just not with her harness.

There were times I sat there and cried, thinking about it.

The fears about being a bad blind person returned, and with them came the doubts about going back into training again. What if I got a bad match? What if I couldn't handle a young, energetic dog? Perhaps the worst of these thoughts was that I was also several years older, now, and the stress might be too much for me.

I was reading a handbook I was editing for a guide dog user group and realized I was accommodating my dog more than my dog was helping me. This, according to the handbook, was the beginning of retirement and time to call one's guide dog school training program for a follow-up visit to determine if retirement was imminent.

I dreaded the call, but made it. As we walked down the street, the instructor noticed a few things—how Verona walked a little stiffly in her back legs, and how I was holding back from overstepping her due to her slow pace. We crossed the street, turned around, and began the walk back home. This was when Verona took me around a phantom obstacle, and the instructor commented that it was time for me to begin the step–down and begin the retrain application.

For a few days, I walked around in a fog, not knowing how to feel about it. Verona was my first guide dog, the only other positive icon of being blind besides my own attitude, but I couldn't just snap my fingers and make the situation all hunky-dory.

I sent up a message to the Big Man in the Sky: Please help me get through this without losing it, and when I do go for my new dog, please let it work out, too.

As prayers go, it all worked out for the best, but not like I imagined.

The instructors did their best to intervene and get Verona moving, but it was as if she had her mind made up: "Mom, I don't want this thing on me anymore; I don't want to be on that loud, rickety bus, either, or go to those conventions where I have to do more than I'm used to doing."

Verona's last effort in guiding me was a testament to her drive to please me, even though I knew it was a struggle.

My sister Cheryll and I flew to California in January 2015 to help assemble some of our mom's legal documents and to stay during her open heart surgery. The trip was extremely stressful for all of us, as it was when we were told that Mom's lymphoma had spread all over her thoracic region and tumors had been discovered on her heart. The heart surgeon informed us gently but firmly that Mom had about six months to live.

We traveled into and out of the hospital so many times that Verona knew where to go without asking. We went on autopilot from the parking lot to the CICU door and into Mom's room without breaking stride. While we were in the room, the nurse would put a blanket down for Verona. The floor was cold, she explained, and the dog should be comfortable.

The visit was hard enough, but we also had a nightmare airplane trip back to New York. We were supposed to leave from San Jose International and take the red eye back to New York, leaving at 10 p.m. The airplane broke down, the de–icing equipment went kerflooey, and since it was the last flight out, we had to pack up and get to San Francisco for the next available flight at 7:00 the next morning.

I recall at one point after midnight getting up to go to the bathroom and having trouble getting Verona up to take me. Then, once inside the lavatory, she got confused finding the way out and just stood there, tail down, looking uncomfortable. I got help outside and pressured her to find the way back to the chair, which she failed at doing, passing it and refusing to guide me back. That was when I knew she was finished.

I sat in the waiting area with my sister and tried not to cry. We were going to lose our mom, and now this? I was just beginning to get my mind to accept that Mom was dying, and while I had to learn to deal with that, my guide dog was telling me she was finished with being my partner. The anger and sadness competed for attention. I didn't know how to face it all without wanting to scream in frustration and pain. My chest actually hurt, and I once again felt the intense heartache of loss and grief that I had after losing our dad.

The rest of the trip was an effort in patience and perseverance, but we got home. I collapsed into bed, and Verona curled up beside me. We both slept for five hours straight. I was mentally exhausted, and I think she was, too.

It was times like that I wished I could read her doggie mind and offer her some comfort in a way she could understand. I will always be grateful for her wanting to be beside me, even if it meant enduring more than a little discomfort. That trip was a nightmare, and I don't recall all of it. If Verona hadn't been there to guide me through the parking lot, hospital, and hotel, I don't know how I would have been able to endure it myself. She was the one I cried to once we were told of Mom's prognosis. She was the one who kept me focused and on task. She depended upon me, and because I had this routine and relationship with her, it got me through the worst of that trip during which we discovered our mom had a short time to live. Being able to retire Verona and still keep her gave me some hope that not all goodbyes meant ending in death. She truly is hope dressed in ebony, and she pulled me through a very tough time.

The poem below is just a small piece of expressing the way in which Verona has touched me. This poem is for all of my past companions, too.

In those dark moments
When eyesight doesn't matter
Where light burns and stars stay undiscovered

The grip of the handle
Eases the panic like a mother's hand
Before the fear rises
Warm nose finds the way down the hall, up the stairs,
    into the store

Like the familiar sounds of morning
The light click of toenails on tile reassures
I grip the handle and follow
The soft jingle of leather and brass
And faint canine scent
Conveys that
In those darkest moments
I am not alone.

Slowing Down

Soon after the trip, Verona slowed her pace even more, and I began leaving her home a few days a week when either Jerry or April was off work and available. Then the days I took her became even fewer, and eventually I was back to using my stupid stick, a.k.a. the white cane.

My retraining papers were in with the admissions department, and I was waiting to hear which month I would be in class.

"If you could tell me what you want to change or get in your next dog, what would it be?" asked the instructor after we came in from the retirement walk.

"Well," I said, "a faster dog."

"What else?"

"I don't care if it's a Black or Yellow Lab. I think I want a dog that's different than Verona. Not just bigger, but personality-wise. Not as cautious. I think Verona is overcautious, and that frustrated me a lot," I said, hoping I was making sense.

"A male is okay?" she asked.

"Yes, I think so. I've had males before, and Nikka is used to big males now that my friend's dog has been here a lot."

I was referring to my friend Mike's retired Lab, Kaiser. Nikka had grown to actually like the huge dog, despite her big dog anxiety. I wasn't as concerned about Verona. However, this was one part of the transition from one dog to the next that I was soon to find I didn't quite understand.

Sure, I'd written about it over the past year, but I wasn't prepared for just how much emotion was involved. I not only had to work through my own feelings, but also had to help my family with the transition. Jerry and April needed to understand the concept in order to help Verona transfer her loyalty to Jerry, and he would have to accept the challenge.

We began by Jerry being Verona's feeder and walker. I kept grooming her, but the daily tasks were up to Jerry from that point forward.

She was confused at first. I could tell by the way she tried to come with me when I left for work, standing by my side while I put on my coat and backpack. I made myself hold back a little over time, prompting Jerry to do and say the things she responded to so Verona would begin to look to him first and me second. He brought her upstate when he prepped his hunting blind. He took her to the beach a few times over the summer. Soon, she was looking to him for affection. Instead of laying her head on my foot, it was Jerry's foot she sought.

I knew it was the best thing for Verona, but it still made me have to blink away the tears. I had to stay strong, though; it was going to make it easier for all of us once I brought home the new dog.

And Nikka? Well, she just went along with it all, bless her soul. As long as she got the best bed and the best bone to chew and was included in the nightly treat, she was happy.

I wrote this advertisement after making the final decision to retire Verona. It really did feel like going backwards, like giving back the independence, even if it was to be just for a little while.

Situation Wanted

A 50–something white female who just happens to be blind is seeking a highly motivated working dog. If you are a Labrador Retriever and are willing to work with me, please read the job requirements. Only serious applicants need apply.

1. Females preferred but will consider a male if all other character and personality traits are met.
2. Height: over 20 inches. Weight: less than 75 lbs. Color: no preference.
3. I am a moderate but steady walker, travel in all modes of transportation, usually in loud Paratransit vehicles or public buses. I also fly at least once a year and commute by passenger train twice yearly. I stay in hotels and motels. I visit cities and live in the suburbs and spend summers by the lake. This means my new partner must be versatile and ready for action, depending on my busy schedule.
4. I will require my new partner to be ready to go from the office to new locations with care and attention. He or she must be able to settle down and quietly observe or ignore my clients and also be willing to offer some comfort therapy if needed.
5. My new partner must be experienced in offering a kind and gentle nose to other furry critters, including cats and guinea pigs and other dogs, as well as children. You will be filling the paws of my current partner, who will be retiring soon. She has been an amazing worker, friend, and part of this community for many years and is loved by all, human and furry.
6. If you have read these requirements and feel that you have the right combination of breed, personality, manners, strength, adaptability, affection, and drive, and you possess intelligent disobedience skills and wish to work with a human who will trust and love you the best she can, please send your contact information to Ann Chiappetta, care of: Guiding Eyes for the Blind, 611 Granite Springs Road, Yorktown Heights, NY.

The day the instructor drove me up to Yorktown Heights was a blur, except for one thing: It took what I thought was a long time to reach out and take the harness from its hook. I was wearing my coat, and my hand was on the suitcase handle. I was supposed to bring back the harness.

I stood there. I couldn't make my arm rise. So many thoughts were roiling around in my head: memories, proud moments, the first time we met. The lump lodged in my throat, and the tears began rolling down my cheeks. The reality of Verona's retirement hit me, and I closed my eyes to get hold of myself.

This is it, I thought. This is what the other guide dog users meant when they said it was such a difficult step. I didn't know what the next three weeks would be like, but I had to grab that harness and, in doing so, leave Verona behind.

I heard a polite beep from the waiting van. Before Verona noticed, I grabbed the harness and left.

Whoa, Doggie!

It was the morning of dog day. I held onto the harness handle. The instructor pulled me along, testing my pace and preferred pull, my correction technique, and footwork.

"Okay, we're going to wait here, and when I come back, a real dog will be in the harness."

I was excited, anxious, and not feeling so good. My asthma was acting up and I felt tired and achy, but I was determined not to give up and go home because of a bad cold. It was March, and it had come in like a lion, cold, wet, and windy. The grip of winter hadn't fully left White Plains and the lower Hudson Valley. Huge piles of ice and snow were left over from a series of late lake–effect storms that had growled down from Canada. I hated having to tromp around in all that while training with a new dog. I had asked to be in the April class, but when I got a call asking if I could switch it to March, I agreed, even though I was concerned about my breathing, already triggered by the cold. But all this was moot when I thought about what was going to happen in the next two minutes. I was going to meet what was most likely going to be my next dog.

The instructor returned with a large, wiggling dog. I put a hand out to let him sniff it, and he nibbled my fingers a little, making me smile. The instructor told me he was a Yellow Lab, male, and about 70 pounds. I gave him a few pats, grabbed the handle and leash, and then we were off at a nice, brisk pace up the street, en route back to the training lounge. I felt the freedom of flying once again, and it felt so good that I wanted to keep going. He didn't have a bouncy pace like Verona. He glided, and the smooth pull was surprising and pleasant.

I did have to stop once going back up the hill, from being out of breath, but when we stopped at the training lounge door, I praised him and gave him a treat. He leaned into me and proceeded to lick my face when I bent over.

"So, do you like him?"

I smiled and nodded. "I loved it. He's faster, bigger, and I like that."

And, that, readers, is how I met Bailey.

We didn't bond right away, and I didn't expect to. Verona had taken a few days to give me her belly, and I thought at the time that it would take much longer for this guy to bond to me, too. In fact, he spent most of the day in my room whining every time he heard his trainer, Stephanie, whom I refer to as the love of his life.

One thing about Bailey: He thinks food is crack. He has a personality to match his large, rangy body and huge ears. He lives to be with people and runs to put on the harness. In other words, he is the polar opposite of Verona. He is faster, has a better pull, and isn't as intimidated by large crowds. Early on, I became impressed with his traveling tolerance. He did not get upset when a bus hit a bad bump or tight corner, sending him sliding. In fact, he is an intrepid traveler.

But we had a very rocky start. The second day of week two, I went home with a respiratory infection that left me gasping for air and unable to walk for more than a block without my chest seizing. After a trip to the emergency room and a chest X–ray, I was wiped out. I remember sitting with the head nurse while she gently suggested I go home and rest. I was exhausted and nauseated, and every bone and muscle throbbed as if I were being compressed with a giant medieval thumb screw.

I cried, agreeing I was too ill to continue. But I was also

fearful.

"Won't that mess up our work?" I asked. "I don't want him to feel like I'm abandoning him."

"He'll be just fine," she said. "You're already a team, and another week of rest won't hurt."

I had my doubts, but was feeling so sick that I let her pack up most of my belongings. After she left, Dell came in and sat with me for a few minutes before taking Bailey back to the kennel.

"Will going back to the kennel make him think I'm gone for good?" I asked, trying not to cry.

"No. Once you're better, we'll finish up your training at home. Just get better, okay?"

I nodded, unable to talk. Dell led Bailey out and I burst into tears. All the old doubts came flooding back—that I was a failure, that I was the worst excuse for a blind person. I couldn't even stay healthy for one of the most important things I needed to do, and now I was going home, sick, without my new dog. I was pathetic, and I felt so alone and depressed.

It didn't enter my flawed thinking that I was burning the candle at both ends. My mom was fighting for her life, and I hadn't come to terms with it. And now I was both mentally and physically drained. It didn't occur to me that I was trying to push through too much at once, that my plate was tipping, and that getting sick like this was a consequence of being overwhelmed by it all.

I arrived home later that day and went to bed. I would be going to my doctor the next day to find out how long I would be out.

Recovering and Impatient

The short-track program for retraining was called the action program and consisted of 10 days of in-class training and five days of home training. Most students were ready to get home by week two, especially if the gap between the retired dog and the new dog was less than six months.

I, for one, was impatient to fly again, having been poking around with my stupid stick for months. I missed the flow and safety of a guide dog, and having been interrupted and sent home was a pretty bad bump in the road. My doctor gave me antiviral and anti-inflammatory medication and increased my inhalers to the maximum doses. The X-rays showed fluid and inflammation in my lungs, and my blood work indicated that a serious respiratory virus had taken up residence and wasn't going away anytime soon. I spent 10 days in bed before I felt strong enough to get up and begin walking.

When I did begin to get back to being in the upright position, my legs were tight and the pain was bad. I called my doctor; he listened to my symptoms and said it was a combination of the medication and dehydration. He instructed me to drink more water and other fluids and take short, frequent walks to get my strength back. Five more days of limping as if my legs were sticks passed, and I began to improve. Finally, I went back to work, and the doctor cleared me to reunite with Bailey.

I still felt horrible and had little endurance, but I was

determined to work through it. I was told by my doctor that the symptoms could take months to resolve because I had a fairly serious case of respiratory viral infection. I just had to deal with it and not overdo it. He said moderate activity was fine, and three weeks after Bailey and I parted, we were together once again.

Jo entered the office. I was sitting in a chair, not at all sure how Bailey would react after being left in the kennel. I wondered how and in what way he would let me know he wasn't happy about being left behind.

As soon as he saw me, he pulled Jo across the room and jumped into my lap, nipping my cheek.

I laughed. "Well, you certainly told me you didn't like being left," I said, stroking his body while he rubbed against me, occasionally nibbling my fingers with excitement.

My heart squeezed just then. I had missed him, and I realized that even though we'd only spent eight short days together, we had bonded, and I wanted this dog to lead me for however long we were meant to be a team.

I talked to him, and he calmed down. Soon after, Jo left, instructing me not to work him to the bus.

"Just be together. Take it easy and enjoy one another."

Those were the best words I'd heard since being sent home without him. She gave me his harness and hugged me before she left.

I was so happy to see him again. His presence gave me hope, something to look forward to since being ill.

It was obvious I still wasn't fully recovered, but Jo let me dictate the pace and work Bailey for the next week. It was fortunate that my place of employment was three blocks from the training lounge. Even after the official training program was completed, Jo came by a few times to help me with a few things. I even went on a night walk, which was very successful, and we walk the route often for practice.

Let me digress here and add a piece about winter and summer protection for dogs, namely boots. Yes, the dreaded dog booties. It is an entertaining and sometimes frustrating necessity because our dogs, who work and accompany service dog handlers during routes, may encounter weather extremes like slush, ice–melting chemicals, and hot metal and pavement. Thus, the dog boot is required.

Imagine, then, being issued these boots and being tasked with putting them on your new dog, then trying not to laugh when the dog begins to react in a very undignified manner.

Verona walks like a duck. Some dogs walk like they're stuck in glue or taffy. Other dogs stand still with one paw raised, and others seem to lose their ability to listen to commands.

This is what I say to Bailey when he assumes a defeated posture whenever I bring out the footwear and ask for a paw. "If I were a dog and I had to slosh through icy water, I think I'd want some protection, right?"

First, the tail droops, then the head drops and the ears hang low, and finally, dejectedly, he allows me to pick up a foot and insert a paw into a boot. He even takes the preferred treat in a way that seems to say, "I'll eat the treat, but I'm letting you know I still don't like the boots."

As if that weren't bad enough, he assumes the duck walk, which is very humiliating for a dignified Labrador. Then he seems to pick up his pace, and I can't help thinking that he's thinking that the sooner we arrive at our destination, the sooner the weird things will be removed.

"It's better than cold feet, right?" I say as the wind whips past my collar and stings my face and cheeks.

He shakes, and I wish I could read his thoughts. My mothering instincts know that his big Dumbo ears are getting colder by the minute. I see that someone has invented doggie earmuffs, and I wonder if I could get him to wear them.

How to Read the Signs

During all of this, Verona was experiencing her own transitional problems. She began to have accidents, urinating on our bed, the floor, and the dog beds. We thought it was a health issue, and after testing and exams, the vets found nothing physical to explain the urinating. We were resigned to having to measure out her water, watch her, and take her out every three hours. This was after Bailey came home with me, of course, and we didn't even think it was psychological, but later we realized it was a stress response to a new dog and my new partner.

How can I express this complicated dynamic to humans? I think a dog would probably identify with this situation much more easily than we humans, but I'll try to describe it.

Verona went from being with me every day, in almost every circumstance, leading us through or past bad weather, dangerous traffic, aggressive dogs, people, and even death. She and I knew how to communicate without talking. A tip of my chin directed her, a shake of my head stopped her, and a smile was the non–verbal prompt for going forward. This developed over time, and trust was the one element that kept it that way. Now I was leaving her home, and she was being fed and walked by Jerry and April. She must have felt abandoned, and she acted out with what was attention–getting, to say the least.

Now, a dog, in terms of psychology, would most likely agree that this urinating was the best action to let us humans know how upsetting it was to be replaced. We did the best we could to give her time to adjust, and she eventually settled into our new routine and accepted Bailey, even when he was bossy and rough with her at times. What can I say? It's the difference between a big, rowdy male and an older, gentler female. She and Jerry became partners, and although it took some time for her to seek his attention rather than mine, it did happen after a few months.

Coming to the door when Bailey was getting harnessed was the one behavior she had the toughest time abandoning. I knew the transition was complete when Jerry went away to a gun expo, and when he returned, she pranced around like a Jack Russell Terrier and followed him into the bathroom and didn't leave him alone.

Second Dog Syndrome:
Blog Post from 2014

Imagine being comfortable with your guide dog, so comfortable that when you step out onto the sidewalk and say, "Let's go to the bank," your dog takes you there, and all you need to do is follow and give hand signals to cross the streets. The trip is completed with smiles and praise along the way. Once the banking is complete, you exit the bank and say, "Let's get lunch," and your dog turns and begins the walk to the deli you frequent. Once you exit the deli, you say, "Back to work," and you bank a left turn and retrace your steps. You are a solid team, knowing one another's body language and routines. The bond and level of trust are so cemented that when you notice your dog begin to slow down, tremble during storms, and startle when a door is slammed, you have to blink back tears. You think, Is this it? Is my dog, at the age of six, going to retire?

For a time, during the first few months following this troubling discovery, it is only detectable on occasion. Then, a few months later, your dog flattens herself on the ground when a truck backfires. A few days later, you are walking with a friend from work and she notices that your dog's back legs are stiff going down a set of steps. Finally, you sit down one night and make the call to the school's instructors' line and ask for a followup visit.

This is not the time to be grateful about being so close to

the school, you think, with a liberal dollop of irony.

A week later, you and your dog meet the instructor, and she follows you on a short walk down the street. Your dog makes a lot of mistakes, which is embarrassing, and you have no explanation because when you are on your own, your dog doesn't do it. Then, on the return trip, your dog swerves you around something that isn't there, and the instructor remarks, "Did you just feel her pull you around something?"

"Yes," you say. "I thought it was a garbage can or something."

"No, there wasn't anything there, not even a manhole cover. That's odd."

You're thinking, This is it. She needs to retire, and she's giving all the signals to tell us.

You go back to the apartment with the instructor and sit down.

For those readers who are guide dog handlers, I am hoping you found some familiarity in the vignette above; I've heard many retirement stories over the years, and mine is just one account. Some dogs fall ill or die suddenly from illness or injury; others retire from the sudden onset of a chronic disorder, like Cushing's or Addison's disease; and still others, like Verona, become harness intolerant. The piece in all of this that is so emotional and so difficult for us to interpret is the bonding and ripping away of it.

For me, I felt that I was to blame—that I was, once again, the inept blind lady who had ruined her dog. It was an irrational way to view the signs of retirement, yet it's where my mind went. Fortunately, the irrationality of it didn't last, and I realized I wasn't to blame for Verona's rejecting her harness. But it was an emotional time nonetheless.

My fears were all in my head. The conversation is short, and the instructor and I agree, based on Verona's recent behavior and her slow pace, that she is giving all the indications that she should be retired. The tears prick at the back of my eyes again, but I push them away. We do the paperwork, and she leaves. I tell myself that this is what's best for my dog and I have to honor it, no matter how hard it is for me.

Once again, I begin another transition, one that my dog would not understand, and I can't hold the tears back this time.

Big Yellow Fellow

Bailey's life began on April 21, 2013, when he was popped out with eight other brothers and sisters at the Guiding Eyes for the Blind Canine Development Center in Patterson, New York.

After passing health and temperament tests, he was given a B name and an identification number, and, after being promised a puppy raiser, he was soon in his new home in Belfast, Maine.

From what I understand, he was an extremely curious and mouthy pup. He ate everything. He chewed everything. He must have been exasperating, I thought, as his raiser, Pat, recalled his antics during our talks. She laughed recalling how big his ears were. He looked so goofy. I wish I could have known him then, held him, and smelled his puppy breath, but knowing someone like Pat and her unconditional love and patience helps me get over not having known him as a pup.

He had his training challenges, as all dogs do. Even docile and obedient Verona was always the first dog to break away and dive into a body of water if it was close by. I recall her puppy raiser saying that if the way to their pond was clear, Verona would jump in.

But back to Bailey. He was and still is what I call a "nibbler." When we first met, he walked around with my wrist in his mouth. He was excited and out of sorts, and this was his way of expressing the stress. We worked on it, and now he rarely does it.

I love his energy, his depth of spirit, and his willingness to work when he knows I've got my treat pouch with me. Yes, he will still work without a treat, but I accept that his work ethic is enhanced by his food drive.

The one thing I say to him is that he'd better work for me for a long time, until he's at least nine. By then, I will be 60 and at that point will require a dog with a lot less energy. Maybe I can apply for a guide tortoise.

Dog Two

He is a sweet yellow fellow
Toasted darker
On ears and tail tip
Gives a nibble and a lick
Golden eyes better than cash
He comes with a snow nose
And personality to match
He's tall and silly
Works, wags, and licks
So far no one's gotten ticked
When he sneaks a kiss.

Guiding me around
Alert and looking for sights and scents
On the bus and on the street
Freedom with four feet.

Bailey with a big stick

2015

For about six months after we began working together, I had some doubts as to whether Bailey had accepted me as his primary person. My doubts were fueled by the times he would think he saw his trainer, Stephanie, and stop or turn his head as if he had just seen a streaker. He was aloof at times, too, choosing to sleep in his crate or on a dog bed rather than at my feet, as Verona had done. He also rejected the routine belongings that Verona had liked in my office, which irked me. I had to switch to a crate in my small office, foregoing the dog bed and crate pad under the desk. Fortunately, shortly after we returned to work after training, I moved into a larger office, and now he has accepted the spot under the desk and a padded dog bed and tie-down in the corner next to my desk.

His resistance could have been the result of our protracted transition getting to know one another. Most likely and thankfully, patience and love paid off. There is nothing quite like a companion lying at one's feet, keeping them warm.

There is also a quirk many guide dogs adopt from the routines learned while in the formal program with the instructors. One is how they have been impressed with the feeding schedule—so much so, in fact, that both my dogs are ready to eat at the same time in the morning and evening. One can set the clock by how accurate Bailey has become. Five a.m. and 3 p.m. are his preferred kibble fests. They were at 6 a.m. and 4 p.m, but after returning from California, he never made the full transition to New York time. Oh, well, you can't win 'em all, especially when it comes to the willpower and determination of a large and insistent dog. I just thank a former United States president for Daylight Saving Time.

I wrote the below and will attempt to honor Monty Python's finest humor. Imagine the voice of Eric Idle or John Cleese as you read it.

> Upon the hour of 3
> Ye canine shall entice the Master
> With four legged antics,
> Frolicking exploits
> And other doggerel
> To thereby convince the Master
> To fill Ye Holy Kibble Pail
>
> Ye canine will not,
> Repeat, not,
> Attempt to entice the Master
> Before the strike of 3 of the clock
>
> Feeding of the canine shall not,
> Repeat, not,
> Be at the one hour,
> Nor the two hour,
> But at the hour of three
> As decreed by the
> Most Noble Master and Keeper of Ye Royal Kibble.

More on Transitioning

Bailey is now my partner, and Verona has assumed a new role. What do I mean? Well, Verona retired in the prime of our working lifespan. We were a well-oiled team. I was finally a confident and active guide dog user, and just at that pivotal time when she should have flourished with me, she broke down. I had to honor that unforeseen divergence with love and care—while at the same time remain hopeful I could somehow be willing to put all of that love and care into another guide dog partnership when the time came.

A good friend I've known for years reminded me, "This is the stuff they don't tell you when you get a dog. If you had known it then, you wouldn't have wanted to do it."

Okay, back to my explanation about Bailey becoming the dog that Verona just couldn't be.

He took a chance on me just as much as I took a chance on him. When we met for the first time on the street in White Plains back in March 2015, he was not even two years old and I was still missing Verona. By the time we stopped at the door to the training lounge, he had given me back what it meant to be a guide dog team. He gave me back the heart and spirit of dog, and by doing this, returned to me what I'd been missing since retiring Verona: freedom.

Here are some other words to describe what a guide dog means to me: confidence, balance, integrity, validation, normalcy, and independence.

We've been a team for two years, now, and he's worked hard learning to keep me safe. He's learned his place in our multi-pet household. He's figured out how to communicate with the cat, too, which I thought would never happen. Bailey is bold, sweet, loving, and goofy when it suits him. He spreads out his toes when he's ready to play or run. He grumbles when Jerry tries to push him out of the way on the bed, and he has a need to place his body on top of you when settling in for the night. He grabs Verona's leather collar during play and tows her around like a reluctant sibling. He doesn't bark and loves to lick. He swims like an otter, and letting him swim and play with Verona is heartwarming to behold. We love and enjoy him, and he is part of our family.

He was by my side when I tripped on a broken sidewalk and fractured my foot, and he adjusted to a slower gait when I used a support cane. He was with me and my family as we made our way through the grief of our mom's passing. He accompanied me to Mom's remains and gave me the strength to say goodbye before she was cremated. He and I spent the mornings during our stay in California after her death walking around the hotel and bike path or sitting quietly in the sunshine. If I hadn't had him with me during that time, it would have been intolerable. His presence gave me a routine, a reason to get through those days of mind-numbing grief. He gave me unconditional love when I needed it most.

Bailey just celebrated his fourth birthday. He has developed into a fine example of the Labrador, and not just in composition. He and Verona have worked together during pet-assisted therapy visits. He has learned how to meet and greet people and pets and even horses.

Below is an essay written about our experiences together.

Our Good Dog Story

by Ann Chiappetta, M.S., Verona, and Bailey

This story began at the time I met Verona, a black Labrador Retriever bred and trained at Guiding Eyes for the Blind. I was matched with her in 2009, and we worked together for six years. When she started to tell me it was time to hang up her harness as my guide dog, it was heartbreaking. She had become such a loving and intuitive dog, helping so many people during our work together. I am a family therapist and also visit schools and other facilities and institutions; Verona was unfailing with her ability to bring a smile and ease the stress of someone who was suffering in some way. She was a dog whose job wasn't done just because her guide dog harness was no longer being used. I did the best I could to honor her doggie work ethic. A year after she retired as my guide dog, she was evaluated to become a therapy dog.

"She's a natural," the evaluator said. "This is just a formality."

After all, Verona did possess an advanced doggie degree, having worked as a guide dog, right?

A year later, we were in the advanced class with eight other teams. Once we passed, we would graduate as one of the official pet–assisted therapy teams for the Good Dog Foundation, http://thegooddogfoundation.org/.

This part of the story will explain the most unique piece in our journey together. Being blind and wanting to work with not just Verona but also my current guide dog, Bailey, and making it work for all three of us was the real challenge. I was anxious and a tad fearful that this trio of blind person, guide dog, and therapy dog would not be accepted by the instructors or the general public. When I got up the nerve to verbalize my worries, the instructor said that as long as I wanted to make it work, there was a way to make it work. Our class instructor was not going to allow me to quit. She made it clear at the very beginning that being blind and having another dog with me wasn't going to be a reason to walk out with an Incomplete or be turned away.

We made it work by preparing and practicing with both dogs and asking for help when I was required to focus on training with Verona. We went to most of the classes with a third person, who sat apart from Verona and me. The helper, either my sister or husband, held Bailey, who stayed in harness. The first two classes were the most disruptive to him, but he earned food rewards for settling and not whining when he saw me give Verona a reward.

Bailey was still young and very attached to me, even after an entire year of being my guide dog. I think his tolerance was challenged when he was asked to settle and let me work with Verona. By class three, however, he wasn't even whining. He settled down and even napped during the last half of the class.

Class four was a test for all of us. I was handling both dogs, and it was a little more frustrating due to the logistics. For instance, the three of us had to work out how to walk together: when to allow Bailey to perform the guide work, and how to train Verona to heel on the right. I felt that both dogs, having been living together for two years and having already accepted their respective roles, were up for it. We practiced for two months, taking practice walks, and the preparation paid off.

In empathy with Bailey and his situation, imagine the person that you have bonded with and guided is suddenly going back to interacting with another dog; I could feel Bailey's confusion. I have since given him some slack but also provided directions and a way for him to perform even when he is not guiding and required to "turn it off." He is rewarded with treats and praise for being quiet and not engaging. He still wants to greet the children, licking hands and wagging his tail, but he will settle when asked.

November 6, 2016, was graduation day, and since then, we have been visiting local libraries. We are now working on making smiles happen. Verona is giving back and helping by being the one to give the gift of positive energy. Bailey has matured measurably in the last eight months, too. I am so proud of his ability to make the transition and step into his harness when I give him the forward command. I am a very lucky lady. I have learned so much about both my dogs and their personalities. It's given me the confidence to go out and help others. It helps me because I am able to give back. Being a person with a disability, I am often the recipient of kindness, and it means so much more to me when I can return it.

I don't know where our path will lead or what the future holds for our trio, but I do know one thing: We will continue to do it together for as long as we can. When I clip on my ID tag and tie on Verona's scarf, it feels like we can conduct miracles with a smile and a wagging tail.

Ann and Bailey, Graduation Day
Guiding Eyes for the Blind

A Weekend to Remember

April 21–23, 2017

© 2017 by Ann Chiappetta, M.S.

Tribute to the First Annual Guiding Eyes Continuing Education Seminar

Like many ideas, It began years ago
Abstracts based upon the past
Concepts blossoming from a common passion.

It was a new idea, unique and untried;
For some, the Challenge instilled apprehension
Perhaps a reason for hesitation
Or for decisions being delayed

For a time, hope came second
As it happened,
Voices united, attitudes changed
Wishes became goals, then actions

The desire to gather together
Was no longer waylaid

Human hearts made it happen
To honor Inter–species relationships
The most powerful relationship of all

The spirit of canine propelled us
To the meeting place.

To 3 days of inspiration
36 hours of memories
And laughs to last a lifetime.

Exuberant Labradors
Stoic and steady German Shepherds
80 teams
30 instructors and staff
40 puppy raisers and volunteers

And really good food
Cumulated in achieving
Cooperation totaling 150%
And energy that could not be measured

A coming together
As vibrant as Woodstock but
Not as muddy.

There were dog tangles
Reunions and tears,
Obedience practice, play time
And Challenges including
A hotel that seemed to be built like a corkscrew.

Faces split in smiles lasting hours
Full Hearts sharing meals
Imagine a ballroom lined with
Classroom–style tables
A person sits in each chair facing the podium
Beneath each place lies a dog, quiet
Or silent, asleep or awake
Snoring or dreaming

Licking a paw
And these canines
Our eyes
Our joy
Our inspiration
Our independence
Our family

Our reason for being who we are
And the reason why we were all there
Elicits an inner glow, a sense of pride
Or accomplishment, or purpose
We know intimately how well
These dogs gave us the ability to soar
Not for only 3 days or 36 hours
But continually.

Our dogs connect us, bonding Hearts and minds
Later, after the reunion
In the afterglow
We will draw upon the link
Recall the shared experience
And, with humble words, thank our Dogs.

Verona, Nikka, and Bailey

Resources and Appendix

List of Guide Dog Schools
in the United States as of October 2017

CALIFORNIA

Guide Dogs for the Blind, Inc.
PO Box 151200
San Rafael, CA 94915–1200
Phone: 415–499–4000
Toll free: 1–800–295–4050
FAX: 415–499–4035
Email: iadmissions@guidedogs.com
Website: http://www.guidedogs.com/

Guide Dogs for the Blind (Oregon Campus)
32901 S.E. Kelso Road
Boring, OR 97009
Phone: 503–668–2100
FAX: 503–668–2141

Guide Dogs of America
13445 Glenoaks Blvd.
Sylmar, CA 91342
Phone: 818–362–5834
Toll free: 1–800–459–4843
FAX: 818–362–6870
Email: mail@guidedogsofamerica.org
Website: http://www.guidedogsofamerica.org/

Guide Dogs of the Desert
Mailing address:
PO Box 1692
Palm Springs, CA 92263
Campus address:
60735 Dillon Rd.
Whitewater, CA 92282
Phone: 760–329–6257
Toll free: 1–888–883–0022
FAX: 760–329–2866
Email: info@gddca.org
Website: http://www.guidedogsofthedesert.org/

CONNECTICUT

Fidelco Guide Dog Foundation, Inc.
103 Vision Way
Bloomfield, CT 06002
Phone: 860–243–5200
FAX: 860–769–0567
Email: info@fidelco.org
Website: http://www.fidelco.org/
To apply for a dog:
www.fidelco.org/prospective–clients

FLORIDA

Southeastern Guide Dogs, Inc.
4210 77th St. E
Palmetto, FL 34221
Phone: 941–729–5665
Toll free: 1–800–944–3647
FAX: 941–729–6646
Email: There is a contact form on the website.
Website: http://www.guidedogs.org/

HAWAII

Eye of the Pacific Guide Dogs and Mobility Services
747 Amana St., #407
Honolulu, HI 96814
Phone: 808-941-1088
FAX: 808-944-9368
Email: info@eyeofthepacific.org
Website: http://www.eyeofthepacific.org/

KANSAS

KSDS, Inc.
KSDS Assistance Dogs, Inc.
(Formerly Kansas Specialty Dog Service, Inc.)
120 W. 7th St.
Washington, KS 66968
Phone: 785-325-2256
FAX: 785-325-2258
Email: ksds@ksds.org
Website: http://www.ksds.org/

MICHIGAN

Leader Dogs for the Blind
1039 S. Rochester Road
Rochester Hills, MI 48307
Phone: 248-651-9011
Toll free: 1-888-777-5332
FAX: 248-651-5812
Email: leaderdog@leaderdog.org
Website: http://www.leaderdog.org/

MISSISSIPPI

Gallant Hearts Guide Dog Center
PO Box 16828
Jackson, MS 39236

Phone: 601–853–6996

FAX: 601–898–4715

Rebecca Floyd, Executive Director

Email: rfloyd@gallanthearts.org

Website: http://gallanthearts.org/

NEW JERSEY

The Seeing Eye, Inc. ®

10 Washington Valley Rd.

Morristown, NJ 07960

Mail:

PO Box 375

Morristown, NJ 07963–0375

Phone: 973–539–4425

Toll free: 1–800–539–4425

FAX: 973–539–0922

Email: info@seeingeye.org

Website: http://www.seeingeye.org/

NEW YORK

Freedom Guide Dogs

1210 Hardscrabble Rd.

Cassville, NY 13318

Phone: 315–822–5132

FAX: 315–822–5132 (call before faxing)

Email: info@freedomguidedogs.org

Website: http://www.freedomguidedogs.org/

Guide Dog Foundation for the Blind, Inc.

371 East Jericho Turnpike

Smithtown, NY 11787–2976

Phone: 631–265–2121

Toll free: 1–800–548–4337

FAX: 631–930–9009

Email: info@guidedog.org
Website: http://www.guidedog.org/

Guiding Eyes for the Blind
611 Granite Springs Rd.
Yorktown Heights, NY 10598
Phone: 914–245–4024
Toll free: 1–800–942–0149
FAX: 914–245–1609
Email: info@guidingeyes.org
Website: http://www.guidingeyes.org/

OHIO

Pilot Dogs, Inc.
625 W. Town St.
Columbus, OH 43215
Phone: 614–221–6367
Email: jgray@pilotdogs.org
FAX: 614–221–1577
Website: http://www.pilotdogs.org/

TEXAS

Guide Dogs of Texas, Inc.
1503 Allena Dr.
San Antonio, TX 78213
Phone: 210–366–4081
Toll free: 1–800–831–9231
FAX: 210–366–4082
Email: There is a contact form on the website.
Website: http://www.guidedogsoftexas.org/

WASHINGTON

Independence Guide Dogs
Located in Seattle, WA

Email: toby@igdogs.org
Website: http://www.igdogs.org/

WISCONSIN

Custom Canines Service Dog Academy
PO Box 105
Sun Prairie, WI 53590
Phone: 844–888–8850
FAX: 1–844–888–8850
Email: info@customcanines.org
There is also a contact form on the website.
Website: http://www.customcanines.org/

Occupaws Guide Dog Association
PO Box 45857
Madison, WI 53744
Phone: 608–772–3787
FAX: 866–854–3291
Email: info@occupaws.org
Website: http://occupaws.org/

Editor's Note

Every effort has been made to provide accurate information in the above listings. Given that such contact information can change frequently, please consult the website of the school you wish to contact to find the most up–to–date information.

Blindness Resources

American Council of the Blind: www.acb.org

American Council of the Blind of New York: www.acbny.org

Guiding Eyes for the Blind: www.guidingeyes.org

Westchester Disabled on the Move, Inc.: www.wdom.org

About the Author

Ann Chiappetta's poems, articles, and short fiction have appeared in both print and online publications, most notably DIALOGUE Magazine, *Matilda Ziegler* online magazine, and other small press reviews. Her poetry has been featured in *Lucidity, Midwest Poetry Review, Magnets and Ladders*, and *Breath & Shadow*. She is also a contributing editor of the last–named publication. She writes a regular column called "The Handler's Corner" for Robert T. Branco's monthly online newsletter, *The Consumer Vision* (www. consumervisionmagazine.com). Her first book was *Upwelling: Poems*, © 2016.

Ann holds a Master of Science degree in Marriage and Family Therapy and currently practices as a readjustment counseling therapist for the Department of Veterans Affairs.

She lives in New Rochelle, New York with her husband, daughter, and assorted pets.

Personal website:
http://www.annchiappetta/com/

Book–related website:
http://www.dldbooks.com/annchiappetta/

To read more of her writing, go to her blog:
www.thought–wheel.com

Facebook: https://www.facebook.com/annie.chiappetta
Twitter: AnnieDungarees

Contact

Email: anniecms64@gmail.com
Cell phone: 914–393–6605

Editing and Self-Publishing Services

This book was proofread and edited by David Dvorkin and Leonore H. Dvorkin, of Denver, Colorado. They also designed the cover, and David did all the technical work required for the publication of the book.

David and Leonore are both much-published authors, with numerous articles and over 30 books, both fiction and nonfiction, to their credit. Four of those books are by Leonore. Her memoir, *Another Chance at Life: A Breast Cancer Survivor's Journey*, is available in ebook, print, and audio formats, as well as in Spanish. The 2012 edition is the most recent one.

Since 2009, David and Leonore have been working to help other authors self-publish their books. Most of their editing clients are blind or visually impaired.

They invite you to visit their websites for full details of their services, the books by their clients, and their own publications.

DLD Books: www.dldbooks.com
David Dvorkin: www.dvorkin.com
Leonore H. Dvorkin: www.leonoredvorkin.com

28255962R00109

Made in the USA
Middletown, DE
20 December 2018